# PRAISE FOR LUCRATIVE LIST BUILDING...

"Glen is without a doubt a 'List Building Genius!' If you want to quickly explode your list and fill your pockets with cold-hard cash, he's definitely a MUST read, MUST hear, and MUST see!"
**—Matt Bacak,** The Powerful Promoter
www.PromotingTips.com

"*Lucrative List Building* is a testament to Glen's profound grasp of email marketing. Internet Marketers everywhere would do well to read this book."
**—Jason Oman**, #1 Best selling Author,
*'Conversations With Millionaires'*
www.JasonOman.com

"I have built my entire online business using list building and relationship marketing strategies. Over the years, I have identified a select few experts in this industry, and having met Glen Hopkins in person, I can tell he is the real deal. Anyone looking to learn the power of list building needs to learn from Glen. His strategies can help you double your profits in 90 days."
**—Mike Filsaime**
www.MikeFilsaime.com

"What you hold in your hands is an excellent email marketing playbook that covers the ins and outs of the game from beginning to end. It's written by a man who, having run a very successful co-registration business for many years, probably understands email marketing as well as anyone on the planet.

Follow the advice in this book and it could probably shave years off your learning curve."

**—Mark Joyner**
Three time #1 Best-Selling Author of *The Irresistible Offer*
and more
www.MarkJoyner.name

# PRAISE (CONTINUED)

"Glen Hopkins is an absolutely brilliant email marketer. His book is jam-packed with practical wisdom and insights that, when applied, will take any business to the next level."

**—Sean Mitton**, Sales Consultant
Founder of www.CanSouth.org

Building an email list is the key to earning big profits, any time you want, on the Internet. Glen's new book reveals the step-by-step secrets I wish I had when I started... which took me years of testing and research to find out. If you want to increase your profits quickly online, grab this book today."

**—Terry Dean**
Internet Marketing Pioneer,
Founder of www.MyMarketingCoach.com

"Glen Hopkins Has Written the 'Ultimate Textbook' for Lucrative List Building.

I have personally used the systems, tools and techniques outlined in this book to build my own highly responsive and profitable list—follow Glen's advice and you can not fail!"

**—Don Mastrangelo**
#1 Best Selling Author, *Ready, Set, Sell!*
www.DonMastrangelo.com

"Building your own opt-in email list is the best form of 'business insurance' you can get. In his book, *Lucrative List Building*, Glen takes his readers by the hand and walks them step-by-step through the entire process of creating their own 'policy' that pays huge dividends no matter what the market conditions!"

**—David Riklan**
Founder of the Internet super-site,
www.SelfGrowth.com

# LUCRATIVE
# LIST BUILDING

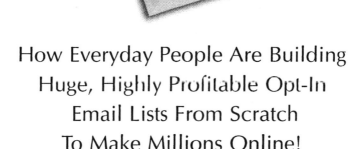

How Everyday People Are Building
Huge, Highly Profitable Opt-In
Email Lists From Scratch
To Make Millions Online!

## BY GLEN HOPKINS

Morgan James Publishing • New York

# LUCRATIVE LIST BUILDING

Copyright 2006 by Glen Hopkins

## Copyright Notice

## Legal Notice

**Copyright 2006 Glen Hopkins, <u>www.GlenHopkins.name</u>**

ISBN: 1-60037-068-3 (Paperback)
ISBN: 1-60037-162-0 (E-Book)

Published by:

www.morganjamespublishing.com

Morgan James Publishing, LLC
1225 Franklin Ave Ste 325
Garden City, NY 11530-1693
Toll Free 800-485-4943

Habitat
for Humanity®
Peninsula
Building Partner

Cover and Interior Design by:
Michelle Radomski
One to One Creative Services
www.OnetoOneCreative.com

# TABLE OF CONTENTS

*continued on next page*

# TABLE OF CONTENTS (CONTINUED)

# FORWARD

By Mark Joyner

Most don't realize it yet, but in the last ten years, the world shifted in some pretty fundamental ways.

Despite the doomsday prediction "the Internet is dead" we all heard when "the dot com bubble burst," the Internet has drastically changed our lives.

Global communication is now universally instant.

Access to (almost all) information is universal.

Anyone can now gain access to a massive audience at a fraction of the cost.

To be heard now, it's no longer required that you have mega-wealth to spend on an advertising campaign. All you need is to be *relevant*.

But alas, it's not that simple.

Yes, being relevant or buzz worthy is the admission ticket to today's global audience, but that only gets you in the door.

The Internet allows anyone to leverage their message to millions, almost instantly, but you need to understand this new medium or any attempts to master it will end in frustration.

Email, for example, is one of the greatest tools of this new medium. With the click of a button, your message can be in front of millions of people.

However, if you don't know the email marketing playbook, your attempts to market with email could leave you with severed Internet access and a whole heap of cyber-egg on your face.

What you hold in your hands is an excellent email marketing playbook that covers the ins and outs of the game from beginning to end. It's written by a man who, having run a very successful co-registration business for many years, probably understands email marketing as well as anyone on the planet.

Follow the advice in this book, and it could probably shave years off your learning curve.

**—Mark Joyner**

Three time #1 Best-Selling Author of *The Irresistible Offer* and more
www.MarkJoyner.name

# FREE BONUSES

Thank You for Purchasing *Lucrative List Building*!

You may now claim your free bonus gifts valued at over $397.00 at http://LucrativeListBuilding.com/owner/bonuses/

# PART I

## Building the Foundation

# CHAPTER 1

## Success Begins in Your Mind, So Let's Start There

Before we get into the heart of this book, understand that if you read what I am about to say very carefully and then do it, chances are you will be earning large sums of money in just a few short months—each and every month.

But all I can do is provide the information. How much money you make is up to you. Only you can determine your success.

If you are determined to succeed, I suggest you model two vital traits of successful people.

## Apply and Test What You Learn

One of the two most important characteristics that successful people share is their constant strive to improve themselves through ongoing education.

Which is what you're doing by reading this book. But don't congratulate yourself just yet. Not until I explain the other half of this education equation.

Successful people are not content to simply learn. What separates them from unsuccessful people is their ability to apply and test what they learn.

Let me say that again: they apply and test what they learn.

You see, knowledge is absolutely useless unless you use it. Does it do you any good if it's just taking up space in your head? NO!

In order for it to benefit you, you need to act on the knowledge that you have. You must, therefore, apply it to your life and your business.

You probably already know you need to apply yourself. After all, how many times did you hear that phrase from your parents and teachers while growing up?

So if the concept of application has been drilled into our heads from childhood, what stops us from applying ourselves and reaching our full potential?

The reason that stops most people is summed up in one word: fear.

## FEAR: Don't Let It Control You

The second key characteristic or trait that successful people share is that they act in spite of fear because they are not afraid to fail. They are fearless.

What is fear, anyway?

Can you touch it?

Can you hold it?

Can you show it to another person?

I can hear your answers from where I'm sitting: "No. No. No."

Okay then, we agree. You can't touch it. You can't hold it. You can't show it to another person. Then why do we have fear?

Fear is nothing more than an emotion or a feeling that we hold in our minds. We fear either the emotional or physical pain something may cause. The problem arises when these emotions and feelings affect the way we live our lives.

We fear doing certain things because we think we might fail. This may be due to past failures we have actually experienced, or it may be due to failures we fear we might experience.

If for any reason you fear trying to build a huge, highly profitable opt-in email list I urge you to remember the following acronym for fear:

**F**alse

**E**vidence that

**A**ppears

**R**eal

Most of the time we have never even experienced what we fear. How crazy is that?

You see, your subconscious mind has a hard time determining whether you've actually experienced the failure or just imagined it. Either way, you feel the physiological symptoms of the fear, such as an upset stomach.

Mark Twain explained it best: *"I have been through some terrible things in my life, some of which have actually happened."*

Often, we believe our imagined failure will come true, and so we don't even try to do what we're afraid of failing at in the first place! That is what makes a failure: a person who is afraid to try because he fears the potential of a negative outcome.

Therefore, you must put aside your imagined fears and go for it! Otherwise, you can never succeed at building a huge, highly profitable list.

## How Do You Define Success?

Who defines what 'failure' and 'success' are?

You do.

Either you create the definition yourself or you accept someone else's definition.

For example, which of the following men do you think lives a more successful life based on the definitions they created for themselves?

Adam: "Everyday that I wake up and am not six feet under is a great day."

Jeff: "I have to be earning at least five million dollars a year before I am successful."

If you guessed Jeff, you better pay extra attention to the next two paragraphs.

You see, Adam has created his own definition of what success means and that definition is relatively easy to achieve. All he has to do is wake up, and he considers himself successful.

Jeff, on the other hand, has decided he cannot be successful until he is earning five million dollars a year. Sadly, most of the 'Jeffs' in the world feel like failures on a daily basis because they are not earning five million dollars a year.

A word of clarification... I'm not saying you should refrain from setting high standards and goals for yourself. If I believed that, I would have titled this book:

*AVERAGE LIST BUILDING "How a Few People Are Building Normal, Sometimes Profitable Opt-In Email Lists To Make a Little Bit of Money Online."*

Who would want to read a book about being average, normal and making a little bit of money? I hope no one because I certainly wouldn't want to write such a boring book.

So what I am saying is that you have to be careful that you 'happily achieve, rather than achieve to be happy.'

The more difficult your definition of success is to fulfill, the more fear you will attach to it; the more you will limit your success.

When deciding what success means to you, create a definition that makes it harder to feel like a failure and easier to feel like a success. That way you will attach less fear to what you want in life, and become fearless.

Imagine what you could achieve if you were fearless. What would you attempt to do if you knew you could not fail?

By the way, I know a secret that guarantees you will never fail again. Want to know what it is? It's simply this: think of every 'failure' as a success.

Every time you 'fail' at something, realize it is actually a success because you have learned what does not work. Therefore, you are closer to succeeding the next time you try.

Remember that the past does not equal the future. Just because you may have failed last week, yesterday or five minutes ago doesn't mean you are going to fail again. Simply learn from what you did wrong and change your approach.

Don't fear the past. The past is what has taught you how to succeed in the future. Be fearless, and put into action what I teach you in this book. After you do, contact me at http://lucrativelistbuilding.com/contact/ and share your success story!

Now that your mind is set for success, let me show you how to succeed.

# CHAPTER 2

## What is Email Marketing, and Why is it Lucrative?

## The Two Things You Need as an Email Marketer

To be an email marketer, you need two things: an ezine/newsletter with relevant information and a list of email addresses. Your ezine provides the information people want and your list provides you with a targeted customer base to market to.

In its simplest form, email marketing is sending your relevant marketing messages, by way of email, to a list of subscribers who have given you permission to do so.

Of course, before you can send your marketing messages, you first need to have a list of people to send it to. Everything you need to know about building your very own huge, highly profitable opt-in email list is revealed in this book.

Note that I said opt-in. That means that the people on your list are 'opting' to receive your information via email. Keep in mind, however, that they only requested information relevant to your ezine.

For example, say your ezine promises healthy recipes weekly. Then healthy recipes in their inbox, once a week, is what they have given you permission to send. So that's what they are expecting.

In other words, they have not given you permission to send them information on 'How to Have a Happy Marriage' or 'The Top Ten Sightseeing Tours in New York City.' Sending information like that would be considered spam because they did not request it, or give you permission to send it to them.

## Why You Must Have Your Own List No Matter What Your Niche

As you now know, having your own list means you have your own targeted audience, an audience that you can build a relationship with. However, you don't want to build just any type of relationship. You want to build a specific type, a one-to-one relationship.

The one-to-one relationship is the only type of relationship worth building. You do so by treating each individual on your list as just that-an individual.

When you write and send a message to your list—whether it be a list of one or 100,000—you want to write it as though you are writing to one person.

The key is personalization. Personalization helps you build the one-to-one relationship. As you build that relationship with your list, they will learn to know, like and trust you.

No matter your niche, people want to buy from people they know, like and trust. Consider yourself.

If you were in the market to buy a phone, who would you prefer to buy the exact same phone from: Marketer A whom you know nothing about or Marketer B whom over time, you've learned to know, like and trust through the emails they've been sending you?

You'd buy from Marketer B, right?

Your subscribers are the same. They are not going to give you money just because you send them an offer. First, they need to know, like and trust you. The type of relationship you build with your list is, therefore, critical.

So how do you build a one-to-one relationship? We'll discuss that in a later chapter. Right now, let's discuss the importance of having a list to market to.

## Why Having Your Own Responsive Opt-In Email List Means You Will Always Have Money in Your Pocket— Even if Your Marketplace Were to Totally Disappear!

The most important part of your business is your list. This is your database of customers and prospects who are interested in what YOU have to offer. They are your very own 'herd' of people who follow you around and want to hear from you, learn from you and eventually buy from you.

After all, you are the person they know, like and trust who provides them with the valuable information, products and services they are seeking.

If you didn't have a list, and your marketplace were to dry up and disappear tomorrow, what would you be left with?

You got it. Nothing. Because without customers, you don't have a business. You'd have to begin again from scratch.

Since paying customers make your business profitable, the first thing you'd have to do is find a targeted audience of potential customers.

But with your very own opt-in email list—one that you have taken the time to nurture and build a relationship with—you'd be in a much different position.

Even if your product or service were to dry up and disappear, you'd still have a list of customers and prospects with whom you have built a RELATIONSHIP. No matter what happens in the marketplace, that relationship will not just disappear.

Relationships, good relationships, last a lifetime. In business, that is the best kind of insurance you can carry. Plus, you don't have to pay any monthly premiums!

In short, the relationships you have built with the people on your list remain, regardless of market fluctuations. So instead of finding a completely new customer base, all you have to do is determine what else the people on your list want and give it to them.

With a list, you still have a targeted audience of existing customers and potential customers to sell to. Having that receptive audience will make it much easier for you to 'start over.'

I'll explain later how to create your own products or services that will sell like hot cakes—guaranteed.

# CHAPTER 3

## From Scratch to Millions:
## The Six Steps You Must Take to Build a Huge, Highly Profitable Email List

In order to build a highly profitable opt-in email list, you must have a solid foundation to build on. That means getting your business online and ready to accept new customers.

Once that's in place, this is the basic lead, capture and sales model I use and recommend you incorporate into your online businesses:

**Send Traffic to Your Website**
*where you...*
**Capture the Visitor's Name and Email Address**
*then redirect him to...*
**Your Sales Letter to Sell Him Something**
*He decides to buy so...*
**Process the Sale via Your Shopping Cart**
*then redirect him to...*
**A Special One-time Offer, Up-sell or Cross-sell**
*then redirect him to the...*
**Thank You Page Instructing Him How to Claim His Product or Service.**

Before you can do any of this, however, you first need to set up a few basic building blocks.

## STEP 1:
## Select and Purchase Your Domain Name

Understanding why you need your own domain name is a crucial first step to your online success. The best way to explain this is by illustrating it for you.

Imagine meeting and greeting potential customers for your pet care business at a seminar. You meet a person who shows interest in your product line and they ask, "What is your Web address?"

You don't have your own domain name, so (after peeking at the cheat sheet you carry in your wallet) you reply, "Please pay close attention. My Web address is www.geotownsfreehosting.com/vancouver/854534/."

What do you think the chances are that your potential customer will remember your domain name?

If they did somehow remember that confusing address, do you think they got the impression that you are operating a serious and reputable business? I doubt it.

The way to fix your problem is simple: buy your own domain name. Then you can tell potential clients that your Web address is something along the lines of "www.PreciousPets.com."

Doesn't that sound a lot more professional?

Isn't it a little easier to remember?

Another bonus of owning your own domain is that you get your own email address. So now, instead of advertising your email address as "John070368@hotmail.com," it can be "John@PreciousPets.com."

The benefits don't end there. Your domain name only costs about two cents a day. For that measly two cents, you can drastically increase your site's traffic volume.

Many search engines will only include you in their results if you have your own domain name. You NEED to be listed in the results of search engines. Search engines are a great way for subscribers to find you, and you want to be found.

Buying your own domain name is one of the best investments you can make for your online business. Besides, after you expense it to your company, it would cost a fraction of a PENNY! I think you get the picture.

To purchase your own domain name check out GoDaddy.com.

Remember, owning your own domain name:

- Increases Your Professionalism
- Makes Your URL More Memorable
- Gets You Your Own Branded Email Address
- Improves the Likelihood of Getting Listed in the Search Engines
- Boosts Traffic Volume to Your Site

But how do you find a domain name when most of the 'good ones' are taken?

Just get a little creative. Try jotting down a bunch of good keywords and piece them together.

Motivational-Messages.com is a good example of combining the keywords of motivational and messages. Since this website consists of motivational and inspirational stories, articles and quotes, these keywords describe key information found on this self-development site.

ListOpt.com is also a combination of two keywords. In this case, however, I created a new 'word' since this website focuses on helping newsletter publishers build their opt-in email list.

If you need some help thinking of a domain name, try NameBoy.com. This service gives you the option to search for and create a domain name using a primary and a secondary keyword, hyphens, and even rhymes.

## STEP 2:
### Find a Hosting Service

Now that you've purchased the right domain name for your website, you need to find a hosting service that will host your website.

You can choose from a multitude of hosting services and easily find an 'economy' hosting plan for less than five dollars per month. However, the problem with such plans is that they don't offer much disc space and data transfer capabilities.

Since you're in the process of building a huge list that will need lots of disc space, you will soon have to upgrade to a better plan that has enough space to support your growing list.

I, therefore, recommend you research and find a Web host that will give you room to grow. Just visit Google.com search for "Web hosting."

## STEP: 3
## Automate Your Business With an Autoresponder

Once you've established a Web presence by obtaining a domain name and hosting company, you need a way to capture the contact information of your visitors and then automatically send them your marketing messages.

The way to do that is with an autoresponder.

Two types of autoresponders send automatic messages: a single autoresponder and a sequential autoresponder.

A single autoresponder works like this: you send a friend an email and instantly get a reply that says something like, "Thanks for your email. Please note that I am currently away on vacation and will be returning on such and such a date. I will respond to your message as soon as I get back."

Most Web hosts provide a single autoresponder service for their customers, but the single autoresponder is not what you want. What you want and need in order to manage your opt-in email list is a sequential autoresponder.

A sequential autoresponder allows to you plug-in any number of pre-written messages and have them sent out at various sequential times as determined by you.

Say you wanted to send your subscribers seven pre-written email messages. With a sequential autoresponder, you could send them on a schedule such as this:

Day 1:      send message 1
Day 3:      send message 2
Day 7:      send message 3
Day 14:    send message 4

Day 21:   send message 5
Day 28:   send message 6
Day 35:   send message 7

And you thought you'd have to manually send each email to each subscriber on your massive mailing list!

A sequential autoresponder is, for the most part, a set and forget system. You create the messages once, plug them into your autoresponder, set the time intervals for having them sent, and presto! You're done.

You get many other wonderful benefits with an autoresponder; benefits that include the ability to personalize your messages and broadcast the same message to your entire list, regardless, of where they are in your sequence.

## Not All Sequential Autoresponders are Created Equal
### The Good, The Bad and The Ugly

You've narrowed your autoresponse search to a sequential autoresponder, but now you have another decision to make. Do you get client-side software, a third-party service or server-side software?

I'll explain each, give my opinion, then let you decide which one is right for your business.

First, is the client-side software. This is a software you install directly onto your computer. That means that anytime you want to broadcast a message to your list, you must have your computer with you.

If you don't think that sounds like a drawback, consider this scenario.

The software is installed on your desktop computer, but not your laptop computer, and you're attending a conference in another country. A colleague at the conference wants to give your customers a once-in-a-lifetime opportunity to purchase his new product, but because your software and subscriber list is only on your desktop, you can't email your subscriber list until you get home.

By that time, the offer is over and you lost a business partner, plus thousands of dollars in sales. Your customers miss out on a fabulous product at a fabulous deal.

Needless to say, I don't recommend the client-side software.

The second option is the third-party autoresponder. This is an autoresponder service you can purchase on the Internet through a third party. These services host your list on their server and give you the login information. You can then log into your account from anywhere in the world and email your client base.

On the surface, this is a great, cost-effective system. But, as you may have guessed, there is a catch.

Many email marketers use this service, and each individual who purchases an autoresponder account through this service sends their messages through that server's IP address. As a result, hundreds of people are sending email messages from the same IP address.

Why is this a problem? Because of spam.

A spammer can sign up for the same third-party auto-responder service that you're on. Instead of building his own opt-in email list, he takes a short-cut by purchasing a list of 100,000 email addresses which have been harvested off the Internet. Then he sends out his spam message.

As soon as he sends out that spam message, several, if not all, of the large ISPs (AOL, Hotmail, Yahoo, etc.) block that IP address because they identify it as a spammer's IP.

Blocking that IP address doesn't just block that one spammer; it blocks all emails being sent from that IP address including every legitimate marketer!

Your messages may be blocked for an hour.

They may be blocked for weeks.

Or they may be blocked indefinitely.

You don't really know because you don't have control over it.

For that reason alone, I believe anyone who wants to build a huge, highly profitable email list should go with the third option, the server-side software.

With server-side software, you (or your programmer) install this software directly onto your Web host's server.

Personally, I use version three of Auto Response Plus. So do most of the publishers that I work with. To check it out for yourself, visit AutoResponsePlusV3.com.

Now, here's the thing. With a service such as Auto Response Plus, the autoresponder runs directly off your server. This means it uses your individual IP address. This is your very own IP address that no one else is using.

So all you have to do is make sure you are sending out good, clean, spam-free email. If you do that, you're safe. You never have to worry about some spammer sending spam email that in effect shuts down your business. You have full control.

You also have control over everything having to do with your email manager.

Third-party autoresponder services put many restrictions on you. One such restriction includes importing subscribers.

If you have subscribers on another list that you want to import to your third-party autoresponder, more often than not they will not let you. However, if your own autoresponder software is set up on your own server then importing your list would not be a problem for you.

You gain many other benefits as well, benefits such as auto-importing. This is helpful if you're using a co-registration service like ListOpt.com because it gives you the ability to have your subscribers automatically imported into your autoresponder.

Many third-party autoresponders will not allow this because they are fearful of spam.

These email addresses, however, are not spam. They are double opt-in subscribers that have requested to be on your email list. Having them automatically imported saves you the time and energy of having you do it yourself.

Okay, now that you've selected and purchased your domain name, Web host and autoresponder, you have the basic tools necessary for creating a successful online business that captures leads, follows up with them, and sells.

Now it's time to integrate those tools in just the right order to make the whole thing come together.

## STEP 4:
## Set Up a Squeeze Page

Now what you want to do is create what's called a 'squeeze page.' A squeeze page is a Web page that is specifically designed to capture your visitor's name and email address. That is its only purpose.

The essential elements of your squeeze page should include a headline for your product or service, bullet points listing the core benefits that your product or service provides and a call to action.

The call to action is your squeeze: ask your visitor to enter in their first name and email address, then click on the 'Submit' button.

In order to get more people to complete the opt-in form, bribe them. Ethically, of course.

An ethical bribe is a bonus of some sort that you offer your visitors as a reward for giving you their first name and email address. As soon as they submit their information, your auto-responder automatically sends them the information you promised.

That information could be a free report, a download for a free ebook, free software of some sort, a teleseminar or something that is of high-perceived value to the visitor, but of low financial cost to you.

To make the bribe work, let them know that when they click the 'Submit' button, they will immediately be taken to the page that will give them the information you promised. That next page, of course, is your sales letter.

One last thing before we move on to the sales letter.

I suggest you include a photograph of yourself and an audio clip on your squeeze page. The audio clip is nothing more than you reading through the text on your squeeze page: your headline, bullet points and call to action. To learn how to do this go to LucrativeListBuilding.com/audiogenerator/

If you want to see one of the squeeze pages I've created, visit PagePersonalizer.com.

PagePersonalizer.com is a service I provide that, among other things, helps you create squeeze pages.

The difference between the squeeze pages that PagePersonalizer.com creates and other more generic squeeze pages is personalization.

When a person enters his name and email address and clicks on the 'Submit' button, he's immediately taken to a *personalized and customized* sales page complete with his *first name and interests.*

In order to create your squeeze page, you do need to have a basic understanding of HTML coding. If you thought I ended that last sentence in a foreign language, don't worry. Simply hire a programmer who knows HTML coding to set up your squeeze page for you.

As long as you have the sales copy already written, a programmer can have your squeeze page set up in minutes. You can find a programmer on sites such as eLance.com or RentaCoder.com.

## STEP 5:
## Create a Sales Page

Once your visitor enters their name and email address and clicks the 'Submit' button, you want that button to redirect them to your sales page.

Your sales page is just as important—if not more so—than your squeeze page. The words on this page are your sales force, so they should be working hard to persuade visitors to buy from you. That means you need to spend a lot of time crafting the sales copy on this page.

If you're not familiar with sales copy, flip to Appendix I of this book for a brief outline of some of the basics. Then study, learn and practice how to write effective sales copy.

Perhaps, however, you don't have time to learn about copywriting or just can't write effective sales copy. If that is the case, then I recommend you either hire a professional copywriter to write for you or do enough research to grasp the basics and combine that knowledge with software that can aid you in the production of your sales letter.

If you're leaning toward the second option, you may want to try LucrativeListBuilding.com/saleslettersoftware/.

This software helps you create your sales letter by asking you specific questions. After providing all the answers and clicking the 'Create' button, the program creates a sales letter for you.

No matter who writes your copy or how you generate a sales letter, a key point to remember is that you should only include one call to action. The more options you give your reader, the fewer the chances that he will purchase your product.

Why?

Because you confused him.

With more than one option, he won't know which product to choose, and will, thus, leave your page without choosing anything. So do not, under any circumstances whatsoever, place more than one link on your sales letter. That one link should be 'Buy Now.'

Let me give you a brief example of how this works in real life.

A few nights ago, my girlfriend and I were extremely hungry. We had been out the entire day and gone a long time without eating. So when we finally made our way to a restaurant and were seated at a table, we were famished.

We were hungry and wanted to buy food. Our stomachs were begging us to feed them. Then the waitress gave us the menu.

Like most menus, it had numerous options. We sat there for almost 15 minutes reading the menu over and over and over again trying to decide what to buy.

Here we were, *hungry customers ready to buy* at that moment, but the many options delayed our decision, and it took us forever to buy.

Here's another example to illustrate my point.

If you throw a stick for a dog, that dog will run, grab the stick and bring it back to you. Yet, if you throw two sticks at the same time in different directions, the dog won't run anywhere. He'll just sit there looking confused. He won't know what to do because he doesn't know which stick to chase.

Since people work the exact same way, only give them one option on your sales page. Do not confuse them. Make your site as simple as possible.

If you make it easy for your visitors to buy what you sell, you'll make money. This is a good thing considering the number one reason you are in business is to make money. If you are not making money, you're not in business.

Before you 'go live' with your sales letter, ask your friends and colleagues to read it aloud and provide honest feedback.

Did they understand what it is you were selling?

Did they understand how to buy it?

Were they confused at any point in the sales process?

I have visited many professionally designed websites of large companies that don't tell you what they sell or how to buy what they are selling. Insane, right? Why take the time and spend the money to create a beautiful website and send traffic to it, only to confuse visitors into not purchasing anything?

Don't let that happen to you. Keep your sales letter simple.

Don't be shy. Ask for the sale.

## STEP 6:
## Follow-up with Sequential Sales Messages

A common phrase in the email marketing world states, "The fortune is in the follow-up."

The reason the fortune is in the follow-up is that approximately 98% of all visitors that visit your website will not take action. They will not buy from you. A good conversion rate on what's considered exceptional sales copy is a 2% conversion rate. In other words, 98 out every 100 people leave your sales page without reading it or buying from it.

Only two out of every 100 actually read your entire sales letter and purchase from you the first time through. That's considered good.

Basically, 98% of the people coming to your sales page leave without buying. Because you've captured their email addresses through your squeeze page, you can follow-up and keep marketing to them.

Studies have shown that the average person has to be shown or exposed to your message, you, or your brand, approximately seven times before they will consider buying from you. Marketing guru, Jay Levinson, figures the average person needs to see an ad twenty-seven times before it has the desired impact. Twenty seven times! Now you know why you see Coca-Cola everywhere you look.

That's why your autoresponder is designed to send out pre-determined sequential messages to your visitors. These messages help you develop rapport with your subscribers so they can learn to know, like and trust you. If you've done your job well, they should eventually buy from you.

So it may take two messages, seven messages, 12 messages or 100 messages before they buy. They may be on your list for two years before they decide to buy from you.

Everybody is going to buy at a different point.

The key is to get them on your list.

That's why you never have to lose advertising money again with autoresponders. Because every ad you place from now on can be a winner—even when you lose money.

I know, I know. You're thinking, "Okay, now you've lost it, Glen." But I haven't. Let me explain.

Suppose you place an ad in another person's newsletter which costs you $200, and you make $20 on every sale.

If you make eight sales, you earn $160.

Gosh, you just lost $40. That's a bad ad, right?

The answer to that depends on how you wrote your ad. Let me show you how losing $40 can actually be a win.

When you create your ad, don't advertise directly for your product. Advertise something that will "bring them in the door." Freebies like a mini-course, sweepstakes or items at exceptionally low prices work well.

The job of your advertisement is to create leads, to get the reader's email address with permission to follow-up.

Using autoresponders that automatically follow-up gives you the ability to set up a completely automated follow-up system for your product or service. You can use three, eight, or even thirty email follow-up messages to generate sales for your product.

Instead of only having one chance to sell to your prospect, you can have thirty opportunities to sell to him—all for the price of one ad.

Okay, so let's do the math again. You paid $200 to run your ad with a link to your automatic follow-up system, and you send seven follow-ups.

You made $160 on the first ad. Don't forget what the guru says—the more a person sees an ad—the more likely they will buy. But for argument's sake, let's say your conversion rate stays at $160 per follow-up.

$160 times seven follow-ups equals $1,120. Now you've made a profit of $920.

Pretty cool, isn't it?

So what do you send out in your messages?

Well, your first message should be a message thanking your subscribers for requesting more information on your product or service, as well as delivering the information that you've promised.

Approximately two days later, send out your second auto-responder message to that prospect. In this message, ask them how they liked their free report or whatever it is you gave them. Also, ask if they have any questions for you.

What you're doing here is reminding them that you have given them something of value for free. Plus, you're soliciting their feedback by asking if they have any questions.

By the way, questions are the best method you have of determining what your prospect's potential objections are. In other words, you can learn why they have not bought anything from you yet. When you can address their questions or concerns or objections, you have an opportunity to sell them.

I recommend sending your third message on Day Seven; seven days after they initially completed the form on your squeeze page. In this message, include more information about your product, and information that highlights the core benefits as related to that subscriber.

On Day 14, send out message four. You could send out an email highlighting the most common questions or concerns that other customers have had about your product or service; then address those common questions and concerns within the email. This is called *managing objections*.

On Day 21, which would be your fifth message, you might want to send out testimonials that you've gathered from your existing customers. If possible, include some testimonials from highly respected people in your field.

The next email you should send is one addressing what may be a common concern of your payment plan. You might suggest that many people have contacted you stating that they were unable to purchase your product because the payment was too high. So you've come up with a special payment plan: "You can make three easy installments of just $47.95 a month."

Then you may send an email seven days later notifying your subscribers of a sale. Perhaps you've got a 'Damaged Goods Sale' or a 'Holiday Sale.' Whatever the reason, just be sure to give a reason.

People need to know why you're doing something. Their response will be much better if you give them a reason why; a reason why you're offering the sale, and a reason why they should purchase now.

# PART II

## The Top Ten Secrets of Lucrative List Building Revealed

# CHAPTER 4

## You Can Build a Huge Opt-in Email List From Scratch

In the same way that you should have multiple streams of income, you should also have what I call 'multiple streams of subscribers.' In other words, you need subscribers coming into your database simultaneously from as many different sources as possible, if you want to build a huge opt-in email list quickly.

To help you develop these streams, I want to share with you the Top Ten time-tested and proven ways to build your opt-in email list.

Nevertheless, these are not the only methods available to build your list. They simply give you a good place to start, and I suggest you use each and every one of these methods.

### The Secrets Revealed

So what are these ten secrets? Simply this:

1. Squeeze Pages
2. Signature Files and Business Cards
3. Viral Marketing
4. Articles
5. Search Engine Traffic
6. Ezine Advertising
7. MasterMind Groups/Joint Ventures

8.  Affiliate Programs
9.  Teleseminars
10. Co-registration

I will explain each of them in detail throughout the next ten chapters. All of them are easy to implement, but some take more time to set up than others.

For instance, the first five are things you can do on your own to begin driving traffic to your site right away. The last five, however, require cooperation with others in your niche.

Introducing yourself to others who sell similar, but not competing products takes time, but as you will discover, it is time well spent. Although you can grow your list alone, the most powerful results come from teaming with others.

It doesn't matter which method you start with as long as you start somewhere. Just read through the next ten chapters in order, then pick the method you like the best and implement it into your marketing mix.

Once you've got that going, add another one. Implement that one and move on to the next one.

Continue to do this until you work your way through all ten.

Then use your own imagination to come up with many more.

Always be asking yourself how you can acquire new subscribers, because subscribers are the most important part of your business.

Without subscribers, you have no buyers.

Without buyers, you have no sales.

Without sales, you have no business.

Keep that in the forefront of your mind in everything you do.

# CHAPTER 5

## Squeeze Pages:
## Squeeze Your Visitors

## The Purpose of a Squeeze Page

As previously mentioned, a squeeze page is simply a page that asks your potential subscribers for their names and email addresses. The way you 'squeeze' this out of them is to provide just enough information about your product or service or ezine to make them want more. So you say, "For more information, please enter your name and email address."

Since the only way to get that additional information is to give you their email address, they do. By clicking submit, they add themselves to your list and are rewarded with the promised information as you then redirect them to the main page of your site.

You may think this technique is silly because you immediately lose 'X' number of potential customers who don't want to enter their contact information.

But you shouldn't care. Why? Because those people who will not give you there name and email address in exchange for your information are really saying, "I'm not that interested." Therefore, if they are not interested enough to simply give you their name and email address do you really think that would have been interested enough to give you their credit card number? I doubt it.

The fact is that squeeze pages do work. People who give you their name and email address automatically indicate to you that they are somewhat of a warm lead. In other words, they are interested in what you have to offer. That makes them valuable prospects.

You don't have to waste time wondering if the people on your list care about what you're selling. You already know they do, because they put themselves on your list.

## How to "Squeeze" Your Visitors with a Special Report

Creating and offering a 'Free Special Report' is a great way to entice visitors to give you their name and email address. This is considered an ethical bribe.

In other words, they will be willing to give their names and email addresses in exchange for a special report that is of interest to them.

You're basically 'bribing' them with this report. Just make sure it is indeed something of interest, content rich, and of value to your potential subscriber.

It can be anything.

It can be an interview with an expert in your field.

It can be 'The Top Ten Secrets on How to _____,' or 'The Ten Biggest Mistakes and How to Avoid Them.'

It's anything you can dream up that would be of interest and benefit to your potential subscribers.

A great way to increase the perceived value of the report is to put it into a PDF or audio format.

Don't have the time (or desire) to create a report yourself?

Then find someone else in your field who's already done it, and is willing to give it to you for free, so you can give it to your potential customers for free.

Why would they be willing to give this report to you for nothing?

Because it is free advertising for the creator of the special report.

Keep in mind that it has to be relevant information your audience is interested in or the ethical bribe won't work.

## How To Capture Names and Email Addresses

All right. You've captured their interest. They want what you have to offer.

But how do you actually capture their names and email addresses?

Two ways: using a Web form created with your autoresponder or using Page Personalizer.

Remember that sequential autoresponder you purchased as part of the foundation of your business?

Well, it doesn't just send out sequential email messages. It also lets you create a Web form that you put on your squeeze page to collect subscribers. This is a great tool to use and just about any autoresponder service will allow you to do this.

This form both enters your subscriber's information into the automatic messaging sequence and allows you to choose the URL for your Thank You page. (That is basically the re-direct page that the subscribers are taken to after entering in their name and email address and then clicking on the submit button.)

Therefore, using the Web form gives you the opportunity to sell to prospects on your website, and the sequential messages gives you an opportunity to continue to sell to them for years following that first visit.

The second method that I use is <u>PagePersonalizer.com</u>. This is a squeeze page 'generator' that takes the whole process to the next level by automatically personalizing the landing page. In other words, when a prospect enters in their name and email address, they'll be re-directed to your sales letter.

This sales letter, however, will not be the same generic copy that every single subscriber sees. Instead, it is now *personalized and customized specifically to target that individual subscriber's 'hot buttons,'* which in turn, dramatically increases sales conversion rates.

I recommend you check out <u>PagePersonalizer.com</u>, but whatever method you use, just make sure that you use some sort of squeeze page.

# CHAPTER 6

## Signature Files and Business Cards:
## Make Like a Dog and Leave Your Mark

Here are two quick, but powerful list-building strategies: signature files and business cards.

## Insert Signature Files on All Outgoing Emails

Now that you're an email marketer, you don't end your outgoing emails with just your name. Nope. Now you add a tag line or postscript after your name on every email. You save this tag line or P.S. as your signature file.

The signature file should include a call to action. Ask the reader of your email if they're subscribed to your newsletter yet. Then provide a link for them to click on that will take them to the sign-up page for your newsletter.

Because of that signature file, they now have an opportunity to subscribe to your ezine, and you have an opportunity to gain a customer.

You can use your signature file on all of your outgoing emails, including your autoresponder emails. Also, if you are actively involved in any discussion forums or discussion boards, you can add it to your signature files there as well.

Be sure to set this up. It's simple and only takes a few seconds. Once done, it's all automated.

## Utilize the Free Ad Space
## on the Back of Your Business Cards

If you're utilizing the free space at the bottom of your outgoing emails to get people to your squeeze page, why not do the same with the free space on the back of your business cards?

This is one 'offline' method that's a great way to build your list.

To make this work, you can either transfer your signature file message to the back of your business card or offer some sort of ethical bribe (a free special report or download of some kind) in that space to get people who receive your card to visit your site and subscribe.

For example, the back of my current business card reads:

*"Who Else Wants To Discover the Ten Most Powerful*
*Secrets of Building a Highly Profitable Opt-in Email List?"*
*Enroll Now and Receive My Ten Week*
*Audio Postcard Course Absolutely FREE!*
*Claim Your Free Course Now*
*www.eMarketingSecrets.net*

As you can see, this is a great opportunity to advertise for free to highly targeted prospects. You already know the people you give your cards to are interested in what you have to say because you've met them face-to-face.

Chances are you shook their hands and talked to them as you gave them your business card. So give these people who are interested in hearing what you have to say, an opportunity to subscribe to your newsletter.

# CHAPTER 7

## Viral Marketing:
## The Kind of Virus You Want To Spread

How would you like to grow the size of your list exponentially with high quality, targeted subscribers that don't cost you a penny to acquire?

Believe it or not, it can be done with the power of viral marketing. Viral marketing is a term used to describe what is also known as Buzz Marketing or Word-of-Mouth Marketing.

Have you ever used a product or service that you thought was so great that you told a group of friends?

Then your friend also thought it was so great that they in turn told a group of their friends?

Then... they told their friends?

So their friends told their friends?

That's viral marketing. Viral, because it travels much the same way as an actual biological virus does: spreading from one 'infected' person to the next. Just like a biological virus, a 'marketing virus' spreads for free, so it doesn't cost you a dime.

Some of the most successful companies on the Internet today are where they are due in large part to their use of viral marketing. Hotmail.com and MySpace.com are two of the largest sites on the Internet and they can thank viral marketing for much of their success.

## Use Links to Spread Your Virus

Have you ever heard of Amazon.com, MySpace.com, or Hotmail.com?

Of course, you have.

Why?

Simply, because they all use varying degrees of viral marketing, permission marketing and one-to-one marketing. But they make ideal use of viral marketing.

How can you model their virus-spreading techniques? Simple—with referral scripts.

Include a referral 'Tell a Friend' link in each and every issue of your ezine. You can say something like:

"If you enjoy our newsletter, and think a friend might also benefit from it, please click here."

Or you could write:

"Please help us share our message with others by telling a friend. It's easy. Just click here."

The 'click here' should be a hyperlink to a Web page with your referral script.

You can find free referral scripts on various sites such as BigNoseBird.com or HotScripts.com.

If you'd like to use my tell-a-friend script for free and make money while doing so, go to: ListOpt.com/affiliate_taf.html.

To see it in action, visit ListOpt.com, and click on the 'Tell a Friend' link.

## Buzz Currency

In his book, *Buzzmarketing: Get People to Talk About Your Stuff,* author Mark Hughes explains that you need to give people something to talk about, something that is entertaining, fascinating and newsworthy.

To do that, you need to push the six tried and true 'Buttons of Buzz.' They are:

- The taboo (sex, lies, and bathroom humor)
- The unusual

- The outrageous
- The hilarious
- The remarkable
- The secrets (both kept and revealed)

When you think about it, this is exactly what all the tabloid and celebrity entertainment magazines focus on.

Many people in the public eye purposely exploit these 'Buzz Buttons,' because they know that they will create a buzz and get themselves in the spotlight.

- The Britney Spears and Madonna 'kiss' (taboo)
- Michael Jackson's plastic surgery (unusual)
- Tom Cruise jumping on Oprah's sofa exclaiming his love for Katie Holmes (outrageous)
- Jim Carrey on any award show (hilarious)
- GM employees telling buyers: "Pay what we pay; not a cent more." (remarkable)
- "I'm not supposed to tell you this but... " (secrecy)

Since there is far too much to cover on the topic of viral marketing here, the best way to educate yourself further on this subject is by reading Mark Hughes' book, *Buzzmarketing: Get People to Talk About Your Stuff* and Mark Joyner's book, *The Irresistible Offer: How to sell your product or service in 3 seconds or less.*

In the meantime, start buzzing about your business.

# CHAPTER 8

## Articles: Build Your List, Position Yourself as an Expert and Sell More... All with the Stroke of a Pen

Articles are a fabulous way to make yourself known within your given niche while building your list absolutely free. But let me be clear. These are not articles you have to get published the traditional way in print magazines.

You don't have to pitch an idea to editor after editor and hope one of them will want to publish your article. You can do it that way, but if you want to build your list, focus on the online publishers of the thousands of ezines on the Internet.

Plus articles make great content for both your own ezine and your own website.

## A Message to Non-writers: Don't Panic!

For those of you who don't consider yourselves writers, I can see the beads of sweat forming on your brow, and those hands shaking in nervous fear. I can hear the panic in your voice as you say, *"How do I write an article? I don't know what to write about? I can't write!"*

If you've never written articles in the past, don't panic. It's not that hard. The key is to pick a topic that is of interest to you, and the words will simply begin to flow.

Now when I say of interest to you, don't forget it also has to be relevant to your newsletter and of interest to your readers. If you get stuck on what to write, I recommend a simple formula: *who, what, when, where* and *how.*

If you answer those questions, you'll end up with an article. Just choose a subject and begin typing answers to those questions. You'll have an article in a short period of time.

For example, say you want to write an article on dating. You might call it, "The Three Secrets To Getting a Date With the Girl of Your Dreams."

Who: "Do you find it difficult to approach women? If you do, you're not alone... "

What: "Read on and discover the three best, time-tested and proven strategies for approaching beautiful women, and what you need to say to get them to agree to go out with you."

When: "In the ten minutes it takes you to read this article, you will have discovered the secrets and have all your friends wondering how you do it."

Where: "There are strategies that you can use in any situation: at a pub, in the grocery store, at the water cooler, in the elevator or at a wedding reception."

How: "Step 1: enter your first strategy."

"Step 2: enter your second strategy."

"Step 3: enter your third strategy."

There you have it. You just wrote an article. Well, almost. Now you have to add a quick summary of what you wrote and add what's called your *resource box.*

You need a resource box, if you want to use articles to build your list.

A resource box is a paragraph tagged on at the end of your article that explains to the reader who you are, what you can do for them, how they can get more information (subscribe to your newsletter), and whether or not they have permission to reprint your article.

Here's a sample of one that I use...

*ABOUT THE AUTHOR: Glen Hopkins specializes in teaching real people how to build a huge, highly profitable opt-in email list from scratch to make millions online. To get instant access to his insider secrets visit: http://LucrativeListBuilding.com*

*Copyright 2006 Glen Hopkins*

*This article may be reprinted provided no part thereof is edited in any way and this resource box is included.*

I recommend that you write your articles in a conversational style.

Pretend that you are writing to a friend rather than your entire list or a massive online audience. When you think in that way, it can often be overwhelming.

So think of it as though you are writing to one friend. When you are writing a letter to one friend or to an individual person, it often comes across as much more personable. That's very desirable as it helps build that important one-to-one relationship.

## How to Promote Your Articles

Now that you've written the article, what do you do with it?

One option is to submit it to the article directories using a fabulous piece of software called ArticleBroadcastPro.com.

With this software you simply cut and paste your article into the program once. It then facilitates the submission process by submitting your article to all of the top article directories in a fraction of the time it would take to do manually.

You can also contact other newsletter publishers who are in similar or related fields.

Other publishers, just like you, get writer's block and don't know what to write. Perhaps they don't know what to say or simply don't have the time to write an article, but they need content.

Hundreds of thousands of publishers out there send out a newsletter on a weekly basis. What that means is that every week they are hungry for content—and searching for it. All you have to do is contact them.

To contact them you'd use similar methods you would when you're looking for publishers to swap ads with or to buy ad space from. (More on that in a later chapter.)

You can also use any search engine, such as <u>Google.com</u>, or you can try the <u>DirectoryOfEzines.com</u>.

## A Way to Provide Extra Incentive for Mass Publication

Providing content is often enough of a reason for ezine publishers to print your article.

But why not give people who are publishing your articles in their newsletters, and on their websites, more incentive to do so?

It's easy. Ask them to sign up as an affiliate of yours and place their affiliate link at the bottom of your article in your resource box.

Remember that little resource box? That's the box that contains a blurb about who you are and what you do and then has a link back to your website.

Why not make that redirect link an affiliate link for the people who are publishing your article?

Then if the readers who click on that affiliate link buy from you, the publisher of that ezine gets a percentage of the sale from that customer.

If you were the publisher and had to choose between publishing an article of an author who's just providing content or an author who's providing content *and* a way for you to make money, which would you choose?

Dumb question, right?

# CHAPTER 9

## Search Engine Traffic:
## Learning to Love Traffic Jams

If you think traffic is a bad thing, you need to shift your perspective.

Today, all kinds of Internet traffic is jamming the information superhighway via the search engines. In order for your site to thrive, you must take advantage of it.

You can do so in two ways: by getting your site ranked for free on the left side of the results pages or by placing a paid ad for your site on the right side of the results pages.

In other words, you can generate free traffic or paid traffic for your website. My suggestion is to create both, so I'll show you how to do just that.

## Free "Organic" Traffic

Free 'organic' traffic is traffic that comes to your website as a result of individuals searching on various keywords related to and/or found within the content of your website.

Therefore, it is of utmost importance that you include good keywords within the content of your website.

You're trying to get into your prospect's head here. For example, what will people who want wicker furniture type into the search engines?

Those are the words you want on your site, because those are the words people type in and search on. When the search engine finds these keywords within your site, they will display your site in the results for the searcher to see.

These keywords should be interlaced in various areas, such as within articles on your website, within the URL of different pages on your website, within the titles of your website pages, and within the metatags.

For example, if you're selling wicker furniture, you should have a domain name that includes the keywords of 'wicker' and 'furniture.' A name like TheWickerFurnitureDepot.com would work.

Now within your site, you should have content or information regarding wicker furniture. Perhaps post some articles that include general information on the upkeep of wicker furniture, how to clean it, etc.

While writing, place keywords within those articles; keywords such as, wicker, wood furniture and outdoor wicker furniture.

Other places to include your keywords would be in the actual URL of the pages. If one of your pages contains an article on how to clean your outdoor wicker furniture, make the URL something like this: TheWickerFurnitureDepot.com/howto-cleanyouroutdoorwickerfurniture.htm.

That way the search engines can see the keywords right there within the actual URL.

Also, include keywords that are related to your site in the title tag of your HTML page. This helps the page rank of your website and Web pages within the search engines.

One more thing; don't forget to add your keywords within the metatags.

You're probably thinking that this keyword thing sounds pretty simple... if you had a way to discover exactly what keywords people are searching for.

Well, GoodKeywords.com lets you do just that.

This is a keyword tool that I use which will help you create a large list of related keywords that you can use within your website.

All you have to do is type in a word and click 'Go.' It then shows you how many people searched for that exact word in the last month.

For more information on keywords, and how to utilize them effectively, I highly recommend John Reese's *Traffic Secrets* course. You can find it at TrafficSecrets.biz.

Another way to build free search engine traffic involves linking.

Search engines favor websites that have numerous inbound links pointing to them.

So if other websites have links pointing to yours, you'll be ranked higher within the search engines. The more links you have, the higher your page rank. The higher your website is listed in the search engines the better.

Now, there are two different types of linking. The first is the reciprocal linking method, or link swapping.

Link swapping is simply when you and another party swap links. For example, I might have LucrativeListBuilding.com and want to swap links with ListOpt.com. So, ListOpt.com adds a link to LucrativeListBuilding.com, and vice versa. That's a reciprocal link.

The second type of link is what's called a one-way inbound link. This is the best type of link you can have because the search engines look upon this with the most favor.

So you want to have lots of one-way inbound links pointing to your website.

These links are not reciprocal. In other words, you are not pointing back to the site that is pointing to you. They are only pointing inbound to your website.

A great way to do this is to use two of your own websites and contact a third party.

For example, at ListOpt.com I might have a one-way link pointing to ThirdPartyDomain.com. Then ThirdPartyDomain.com would have a one-way link pointing to LucrativeListBuilding.com. Now both ThirdPartyDomain.com and LucrativeListBuilding.com have a one-way inbound link to them. I can even take it a step further and have a link on <u>LucrativeListBuilding.com</u> pointing to <u>ListOpt.com</u>.

There's no reciprocal linking here, only one-way inbound links.

Of course, before you can do any of this, make sure that your actual website is listed in the search engine. To do this, I recommend going to each individual search engine and submitting your URL. Do this manually.

Do not use search engine submission tools that help you submit your domain name or website to multiple search engines at the same time or automatically.

Search engines do not like this. They track it. They can see it. Often times, they will ban your website or not allow it into their search engine listings, if you use a search engine submission software tool. So be sure to do that by hand.

## Pay Per Click

Remember that list of keywords you created to scatter on your website?

Good. Now you're going to use them to generate instant, cheap traffic for your website.

Using Pay Per Click advertising, you bid for keywords. If your bid is the highest, then your ad gets listed at the top of the right side of the results page when someone searches for that particular word.

For example, if you have a website that sells lamps, you might purchase search terms like lamp, light, desk lamp, light bulbs, etc.

For each of these terms, you bid for the position of your listing on the right side of the search engine—the highest bidders are at the top.

The more popular the word, the more it costs to get your ad at or near the top.

One of the best Pay Per Click search engines is Google AdWords. If you are not already taking advantage of Google and the amount of traffic they can bring to your site, you need start right now.

Many people visit the site and search for everything you can possibly imagine. Including what it is you sell.

So take a moment now to set up your AdWords account, and start advertising with them. You'll bring in a ton of traffic and build a huge list of targeted subscribers.

When they click on your ad and come to your site, what are they going to do?

You got it. Sign up for your newsletter. And eventually buy from you.

# CHAPTER 10

## Ezine Advertising:
## Other People's Influence

Ezine advertising is a great way to build your list. It can be done in a number of ways, including cross-pollinating your lists, buying ad space in other ezines, and swapping ads.

When you advertise in ezines, target your marketing as much as possible by choosing content-related ezines. For example, to sell lamps, you might choose an interior decorating ezine, but not a sports-related ezine.

Also, ask the owner of the ezine to read and endorse your newsletter. This will do wonders for your conversion ratio, because the readers already trust the opinion of the ezine publisher. That publisher, in essence, transfers their credibility to you by endorsing your ezine to their readers.

## Cross-Pollinate Your Own Lists

If you have two or more related newsletters, you should cross-pollinate. What I mean is that you should recommend to the subscribers of one newsletter that they also subscribe to the other.

Now this will only work if the newsletters are related in some way.

Hey, why not do this?

You've already got an audience of subscribers who listen to what you have to say. Chances are they want to hear more. They're looking for content, so provide it to them.

## Buy Ad Space in Other Ezines

Another way is to buy ad space using three different types of ads.

You can buy a sponsorship ad. This is typically at the top of the publisher's newsletter above their main content.

You can buy a classified ad. This is typically at the bottom of the publisher's newsletter below their main content.

Or you can buy a solo ad, which is just that. It's an ad that the publisher would send on your behalf to their list advertising your newsletter.

## Joint Venture with Ad Swaps

Finally, you can do an ad swap with other publishers that have the same or similar content. They run your ad, but instead of you paying them for advertising space, you run their ad in your newsletter. It's an even swap.

To find these joint venture partners, seek out other publishers in a related field. All you have to do is go to a search engine such as Google and type in your keywords.

If, for instance, you have a newsletter about interior decorating, just type 'interior decorating' into the search box. Once you click search, a list of different sites related to interior decorating will appear. Then visit those sites one by one.

On sites that look like they promote good information, contact the Webmaster and ask if they would like to work with you. Chances are they will. After all, they are in the same situation as you and are looking to build their list as well. If they're not, that's fine. Just move on to the next site.

If the search engine method is too tedious for you, try the Directory of Ezines (DirectoryOfEzines.com). This is a site, which consists of hundreds, possibly thousands, of newsletter publishers who are looking to buy, sell and swap newsletter ads.

You can reach over 27 million readers in the ezines listed in the Directory of Ezines. The time you'll save is well worth the very small fee they charge for access to their searchable database, so it's worth taking a look at.

# CHAPTER 11

## The Math Equation
## They Never Taught You in School

## MasterMind Groups:
## How To Multiply Your Results With Less Effort

Do you know what one plus one equals?

If you answered 'two,' then I want you to do a little exercise right now.

Raise both hands and extend your index fingers.

Come on. Try it. It won't hurt.

Good. Now bring your two index fingers together.

What number do you see?

That's it! Eleven!

Such is the power created by forming a MasterMind Group. Because two minds are not only better than one—they are better than ten.

For years, successful entrepreneurs have taken advantage of the leverages that MasterMind Groups can offer.

Belonging to a MasterMind Group can accelerate your business growth, increase your personal wealth, and help you to live the life that you truly deserve.

Most people search for years looking for gold, but often, the wealth is right under their nose. You see, when you put your head together with just one other success-focused entrepreneur, your ideas don't just double, they multiply exponentially.

The concept of the MasterMind Group was first introduced by Napoleon Hill in the early 1900s. In his timeless classic, *Think And Grow Rich* he explained the MasterMind as:

"The coordination of knowledge and effort of two or more people, who work toward a definite purpose, in the spirit of harmony."

He continues...

"No two minds ever come together without thereby creating a third, invisible, intangible force, which may be likened to a third mind."

The MasterMind, thus, gives you a way to learn, understand and apply much more than you know now—at a much faster rate than trying to figure it out yourself.

Let's face it. You don't know it all. Neither do I. That's why entrepreneurs need to help each other by forming MasterMind Groups.

One of the best ways I have found to create a MasterMind Group is through networking. Effective networking, in my opinion, is best accomplished by attending workshops and seminars in your field of interest.

Recently, I spent five days in San Antonio, Texas, where I caught up with a bunch of friends and colleagues while creating many new ones.

These new friendships will turn into MasterMind Groups and business partnerships that will inevitably take my business to the next level.

You can take a peek at some of the pictures at GlenHopkins.name/pics/.

The more you get to know like-minded people in your industry, the better the chances are of forming a powerful MasterMind Group.

Although your MasterMind Group will be made up of like-minded people, such as entrepreneurs with marketing savvy, each individual in the MasterMind Group should have different skill sets to bring to the table.

For example, if you are an Internet marketer like myself, you might want a computer programmer, a graphic designer, a copywriter, and a sales professional in your group. This way, each of you can approach a challenge from a different perspective and offer valuable insight that the others would never have seen.

Once you have created a MasterMind Group, it is important to meet with them on a regular basis. This can be done by telephone, online or in person.

I like to meet at least once every week or two to discuss where we are on various projects, where we need to go, and how to get there. The frequency in which you meet should be scheduled to ensure accountability.

Because most of my MasterMind Group lives around the world, we usually meet by telephone or online via an Online MasterMind such as <u>ListOpt.com/mastermind</u>.

I suggest you do some research and learn as much as you can about MasterMind Groups. Start now by networking and meeting with other people. Then use the power of one plus one, and you'll create your own powerful MasterMind Group in no time.

Your MasterMind Group will fast become an invaluable tool for you to meet, brainstorm and Joint Venture with some of the most successful entrepreneurs on the Internet today.

The opportunities that you'll uncover while MasterMinding and casually chatting with other like-minded individuals will help you get your ideas off the ground and to the marketplace faster than ever.

## Joint Ventures (JV's)

The best method I know of to multiply your online results, such as doubling the size of your opt-in email list or increasing your sales, is through the use of joint ventures.

Joint ventures are partnerships created with other reputable business people that create a win-win situation for not only you and the person you partner with, but with your customer as well.

Typically, each party takes on defined roles and responsibilities in a given project and shares in both the costs and benefits.

A simple 'ad swap' whereby each party advertises or recommends the other's product or service in their respective newsletter could be considered a joint venture.

The key, of course, is to always send traffic to your squeeze page in order to capture the visitor's name and email address and, therefore, build your list.

Here's how you do it.

Create a subscription page for your newsletter. Once the visitor subscribes to your ezine, have them automatically forwarded to a 'Thank You' page that offers your partner's ezine along with a recommendation. (The recommendation will greatly improve the response you get, so give your partner a good one.)

Now all you have to do is have your partner do the same thing. Provided you are both generating approximately the same amount of new subscribers per day, you will DOUBLE your subscription rate.

The key to getting a good conversion is your sales copy. (For a crash course on How to Write Professional Ad Copy that works, see Appendix I.) Like anything, you need to be able to sell what it is that you are offering—even when you are offering something for free, such as a newsletter.

Another type of joint venture is in the form of a personal endorsement that each partner sends out to his respective ezine readers. This technique yields amazing results.

What you want to do is work out a deal with your joint venture partner whereby you can offer his subscribers a special offer or discount for your product or service.

By doing this, your partner wins because he is making his readers an exclusive offer (which means the subscriber wins, too). Your partner may also reap the rewards of any referral fees you might give him.

You win because all this new business is generated for you for free!

Below is a sample of a joint venture endorsement letter that a partner of mine sent out to her entire subscription list. I, in turn sent out a similar letter to my subscribers. The letter will give you a clear picture of how you can implement this technique right away:

Sample Joint Venture Letter

*Dear Friend,*

*Why would I be writing to you about a subscriber acquisition service?*

*It's because I felt it was so important that you find out about The ListOpt List Builder Service. You know, there aren't too many businesses nowadays that meet your expectations, let alone exceed them. But ListOpt Publications has done just that.*

*And that's why I wanted to personally introduce you to Glen Hopkins, the owner of* <u>*ListOpt.com*</u>

*For four years now, Glen has collected tens of thousands of opt-in email addresses for my ezine and has been an absolute pleasure to do business with.*

*Since I'm always on the look out for great deals for my valued subscribers, friends and fellow ezine publishers, I asked Glen if he could let me do something special for you.*

*After a bit of friendly persuasion, he agreed!*

*So here's the deal. When you join The ListOpt List Builder Service and forward this letter to Glen, you'll get five dollars added to your account credit. I've attached information below so you could see what Glen has to offer.*

*Take a look at it, and then contact Glen at Glen@ListOpt.com right away. You'll be glad you did.*

End Sample Joint Venture Letter

Here's another sample in the form of a postscript:

> *"P.S. By the way, if you're interested in learning more about*
> _____*, I recommend you check out my friend's newsletter*
> *at <u>www.JaneDoeNews.com</u>. I have been a subscriber and avid*
> *reader of Jane's for over a year now, and have learned a ton."*

Can you see the potential in doing something like this?

The reason joint ventures are so powerful is leverage. When your partner recommends you to their list, you gain instant credibility in the eyes of the people on their list.

When you acquire a new subscriber in any other circumstance, you need to take the time to build rapport before they know, like and trust you enough to buy from you.

But when your JV partner personally recommends you to their list of subscribers and customers, whom they have already built a rapport with, a transfer of credibility takes place.

A more complex form of a Joint Venture involves the use of an affiliate program whereby one or both partners get paid an affiliate commission from the sales of any referred business.

In the promotional campaign for this book, I contacted a number of joint venture partners, who were glad to help me with the sale of this book for three main reasons:

1. They liked the book and believed it was of value to their subscribers and customers.
2. My sales process gave them the opportunity to build their lists.
3. Each time a customer purchased my one-time offer, they got paid a commission.

The key to getting other people to agree to work with you is to ASK.

If you don't ask, you don't get. Period.

If you're sitting around waiting for other people to come to you, you'll be waiting for a long time.

Therefore, at some point, you have to get out there and ask people to joint venture with you. Some will say yes. Some will say no. Be prepared for either answer.

I will, however, share two great ways right now that will help increase the chance that your potential JV partner will agree to venture with you in business:

1. Make the process very simple. Then do everything and anything you can to simplify the process further. The less work they have to do, the better the chance that they will do it. Sign them up for your affiliate program yourself, write the sales copy for them and give them a step-by-step checklist of things to do.

2. Let them know what's in it for them. If they don't know how they will benefit, chances are they will not participate. Therefore, do your utmost to share with them all the benefits they will receive—and make them good!

Will they build their list?

Get a handsome commission?

Build their reputation?

Gain traffic to their site?

Whatever it is, tell them what's in it for them. The more they stand to benefit, the better the chance they will want to work with you.

## Six Degrees of Separation

Whether you realize it or not, you probably already know the people who will become your JV partners. If you don't, one of your friends or colleagues knows the person you want to get in contact with. Or they know a person who knows a person, etc.

It is your job to network and get people to introduce you to the people they know.

A great place to start searching for JV partners and networking in general is within your own MasterMind Group. You can also attend seminars, workshops, tele-classes and meetings at your local Chamber of Commerce.

And, of course, you can search the Internet for potential JV partners in your niche and introduce yourself.

Keep in mind that developing good JV partnerships is much like building a responsive list. You need to develop some rapport and build relationships. The more solid your relationship with an individual, the better the chance they will be willing to work with you.

# CHAPTER 12

## Affiliate Programs:
## Build an Army

Would you like to have hundreds or thousands of sales people working for you?

People who sell your products and services?

People you never have to pay a salary or benefits to?

People that make you money instead of cost you money?

If you think this sounds too good to be true, think again.

## What is an Affiliate Program?

An affiliate program is what I have just described above. It's a program that allows other people to sell your products or services for you.

The ONLY time you pay them is when they make a sale. In other words, they make you money, then you pay them a commission. It's called ZERO cost sales and marketing.

When people join your affiliate program, they promote your products and services on their time and at their expense. They do it because they know that if they do it well, you will pay them a commission.

The great thing about affiliates is that they help you spread your reach far, far beyond what you could ever do on your own.

Say you had your own list of 10,000 subscribers and no affiliates. Basically, you'd only have 10,000 potential customers that you could market to.

But if you had just one affiliate who also had a list of 10,000 subscribers, you would immediately double your reach.

So what if you had five affiliates, ten affiliates or 100 affiliates? It's possible. In fact, many people on the Internet today have thousands of affiliates.

Not all affiliates are going to be equal in that some will perform better than others. These are called your super affiliates, and you want to pay close attention to your super affiliates.

Be sure to reward them differently than you reward others because these are the people that will bring in the vast majority of your business.

## The Way to Build Your List Using Affiliates

In order to use affiliates to build your list, you need to remember that any and all traffic that you send to your site should be sent to your squeeze page. That means your affiliates are sending the traffic they generate to your squeeze page.

As you already know, you're going to collect the visitor's first name and email address on that squeeze page. Once you've collected that information, you send them to the next page where they have the opportunity to purchase your product.

Thus, you are building your list and you now have the opportunity to follow-up with those 98% who don't buy the first time they see your sales message.

By capturing their first name and email address, you have an opportunity to market to them over and over again.

The more you market to them, the more you build your relationship with them, and the better the chances are that they will eventually buy from you.

This, of course, benefits both you and your affiliates.

With the use of a proper affiliate program, you can use cookies to track where your subscribers are coming from.

If your affiliate sent you a subscriber who turned into a customer months later—possibly a year later depending on how far you have your cookie set—that affiliate will still get paid a commission on everything that subscriber buys.

So both you and your affiliates benefit if you send all traffic through your squeeze page.

You will soon find that as your army of affiliates grows, your traffic will grow so much so that you gain an unstoppable flow of traffic—traffic that you are not paying for.

Keep in mind that your affiliates are working for you for free. They are promoting your products through email, on their websites, or on their blogs.

Some affiliates, such as super affiliates, will often pay to advertise your product or service knowing that the return on investment will be positive for them.

For example, many affiliates will purchase Pay Per Click search engine traffic and forward that traffic through their affiliate link to your site, making both you and the affiliate money.

It's easy to see that having your own affiliate program can drastically increase your profitability in a very short period of time. In fact, most Internet marketers and sales people will tell you that the majority of their income comes via their affiliates.

## How to Create Your Own Affiliate Program

You can create your own affiliate program in three basic ways.

First, you can use a third party affiliate program. All you have to do is visit one of the major search engines such as Google and type in 'affiliate programs.' A list of various services that offer affiliate programs will pop up. Typically, they'll charge you a small monthly fee.

The second option is to purchase affiliate software. Again, you can do a search on the major search engines to find your own server-side software. Having your own server-side software does give you more flexibility, and it is only a one-time payment.

The third option is what I call 'in house software,' or software that you have specifically designed and programmed to suit your needs. If you don't know programming, you would have to hire a programmer. They are easy to find at places such as Elance.com or Rentacoder.com.

Note: When you have your own in house affiliate program or server-side affiliate program, the affiliate links will all run directly through your domain name or your URL.

As your affiliate army grows and these affiliates paste their unique affiliate links on their websites and blogs, they will, in effect, be advertising for you for free and creating one way, inbound links pointing to your domain.

As you know, the more one way, inbound links that you have pointing to your domain, the better your search engine rankings will be. This is a very, very favorable position to be in.

# CHAPTER 13

## Teleseminars:
## Building Your List at the Speed of Sound

While sitting at home with not much equipment other than your phone, you can build a list of qualified and instantly responsive subscribers literally at the speed of sound.

All you need to do is host a teleseminar.

## What You Need
## to Host a Teleseminar

The only equipment you need to host your own teleseminar is a phone and a bridge line to allow other callers to dial in and attend the call. Several bridge line services are available for your use, including free services such as <u>FreeConferenceCall.com</u>.

By the way, some bridge line services offer recording abilities while others do not. So if you're using a service that doesn't have recording abilities, but want to record the call, you can hire a professional recording and editing service such as <u>RecordedMoments.com</u>.

Or you can purchase your own audio recording equipment from experts at <u>LucrativeListBuilding.com/audio-equipment/</u>.

## Let Prospects Listen to a Phone Conversation Between You and an Expert in Your Field

You can host many different types of teleseminars, but the easiest and best method for using them to build your list is to interview other experts in your field. This way, both the subscribers on your list and the subscribers on your guest's list will be interested in listening to the call.

For list-building purposes, create a call registration page where all attendees must register to be on the call.

Relax. This isn't something new you have to learn how to do. Because your registration page is nothing more than a 'squeeze page' used to capture your registrant's name and email address.

The beauty of this process is that extremely targeted prospects add themselves to a new 'sub-list' for you.

To show you what I mean, let's say your main list is for your newsletter, *Interior Design for the Weekend Enthusiast*, and the topic of the teleseminar is "How To Paint Your Bedroom In Two Hours Flat From Start To Finish."

Those who want to learn about painting sign up for the call.

Now you have two lists. Your main list, *Interior Design for the Weekend Enthusiast*, and a sub-list of people who have shown a special interest in how to paint. This allows you to market 'paint' related products and services to your new, highly targeted sub-list.

The overall process of building your list looks like this:

1. Contact an expert to interview and determine the subject of the call.
2. Both you and your guest expert email your respective lists announcing the free teleseminar.
3. Interested subscribers register for the call by giving you their name and email address on the Call Registration page.
4. When they submit their contact information, they are redirected to a 'Thank You' page which contains the details of the teleseminar.

You can see an example of this process in action at AskTheMaster.net/andy/.

Keep in mind that this call has already taken place. If you want to hear the replay, visit: AskTheMaster.net/andy/replay/.

Another wonderful thing about teleseminars, is that you have the opportunity to build instant rapport with your audience.

During a very short period of time (most teleseminars are about one hour long), you capture the attention of every listener on the call.

If you do your job right, many of them will learn to know, like and trust you. Often this is because your listeners will be able to identify with you on some level.

In addition, your listeners now see you as more of an expert in your field because you shared some of your knowledge with them. And by interviewing another expert in your field, his or her credibility is transferred onto you by way of association.

Many marketers use teleseminars to educate their listeners on a topic for the majority of the call. Then, after providing great content and value, they sell the listeners their products or services.

# CHAPTER 14

## Co-Registration: How to Build Your List from Scratch in Less Than Ten Minutes

## How To Build Your List From Scratch in Less Than Ten Minutes

Of all the list building strategies discussed, co-registration is by far the fastest way to build your opt-in email list.

What, you ask, is co-registration?

Well, it's when one person or organization advertises two or more offers at the same time. A visitor can then choose to register for more than one newsletter simultaneously.

If you don't have a lot of time to spare, and you want to build your list quickly, easily and inexpensively, take a look at what top Internet marketer's such as Mark Joyner, Key Evoy, Tellman Knudson, and Matt Bacak recommend: ListOpt.com/listbuilder/.

With List Builder, you can get as many as 2,000 targeted, double opt-in subscribers each and every month, with no effort on your part. These subscribers are all double opt-in and specifically request a subscription to your newsletter.

How cool is that?

## Revenue Generation: 101

Pop quiz: Does size really matter?

    A:  Yes
    B:  No
    C:  Depends
    D:  All of the above

At first glance, the answer (or my answer) may seem obvious; of course, I'd choose A since I am known as 'The List Builder Guy' who helps people build huge, opt-in email lists.

But A is not the best answer. If you were to answer B or C, you'd also be right. Therefore, the most correct answer is D: all of the above.

Allow me to explain...

The two key elements in any opt-in email list are quantity and quality.

Let's discuss quantity first.

Nobody with any sense could argue the simple fact that you will have more conversions with larger lists.

Think of a list like a fishing net. Assuming all other factors are equal, the person with the larger net is always going to catch more fish than the person with the smaller net.

This is why marketers often refer to sales as a 'numbers game.' So let's look at this numbers game in action.As you now know, size does matter when it comes to your opt-in email list. Without a sizeable list, the quality of your list won't mean much.

According to the industry standard, a two percent conversion rate is considered excellent.

Based on that, let's say you sell a product for $97 to a list of 100 subscribers. At a 2% conversion rate, you'll make $194.

100 subscribers x 2% conversion rate = 2 buyers
2 buyers x $97 = $194

Okay, now let's say you sell the same $97 product to a list of 1,000 subscribers. At the same 2% conversion rate, you'd make $1,940.

1,000 subscribers x 2% conversion rate = 20 buyers
20 buyers x $97 = $1,940

Don't you agree that's a pretty nice increase in revenues? But to be fair, let's deduct the cost of purchasing the extra 900 subscribers based on the current subscriber cost of $0.29 each at ListOpt.com/listbuilder/.

So here's the math:

900 purchased subscribers x $0.29 = $261

Back to our example. Two people from the original 100 bought your product, so we'll deduct that from the total revenue:

$1,940 total from list of 1,000—$194 from original 100 = $1,746

Take the revenue generated by the extra 900 subscribers you bought and deduct the purchase price:

$1,746 total from extra 900—$261 cost to buy extra 900 = $1,485

Having an extra 900 subscribers made you an additional $1,746 in gross sales and an extra $1,485 in net sales!

Now let's discuss quality.

Not all lists are created equal. If you are ever given the opportunity to advertise in a list of 100,000 *subscribers* versus a list of 1,000 *buyers*, you should always choose the list of 1,000 buyers.

A list of buyers is a list of subscribers who have proven that they:

- Are reading your email.
- Are interested in what you have to say.
- Have a credit card.
- Are willing to buy from you.

This is the most powerful list you can own—a list of existing customers or buyers. With that in mind, it is important that you segregate your lists.

To do this, you start with your general list of subscribers. As soon as one of your subscribers purchases a product or service of yours, you should automatically move them to your buyer's list. Now you have two lists: your general list and your buyer's list.

Your buyer's list is your all-important gold mine.

But here's the really cool thing. You only have to buy or acquire a subscriber once.

That same subscriber, if treated right, can become your *lifetime* customer and put cash in your pocket over and over and over again.

Building a large opt-in email list is the easy part. It can be done for you on autopilot using List Builder at ListOpt.com/listbuilder/. The harder part is creating a highly *responsive* opt-in email list.

As you build the size of your list, you need to constantly nurture it. The more you care for it, the more quality fruit it will produce.

The secret to building a quality list of highly responsive subscribers is... drum roll please...

... Relationships!

By taking the time to build a relationship with your subscribers, they learn to value your opinion. Only then, will they consider buying something from you.

The best way to develop a strong relationship with your readers is by constantly providing them with valuable information and services. By doing this, you build a sense of rapport, and your subscribers learn to see you as an expert in your field-an expert that they know and trust.

Now let's take that quiz again.

Does size matter?

A. Yes, because quantity equals more sales. Duh.

B. No, because only quality subscribers respond and make me money.

C. Depends, because I need both quantity and quality to build a lucrative list.

D. All of the Above, because I understand that building relationships is the key to achieving that important balance between quantity and quality.

The answer: D.

Great job. You passed the quiz. You have now graduated from List-building School and are ready to enter Lucrative List University. Here you will learn how to make millions online.

If that interests you, read on.

# PART III

## Turning Subscribers Into Customers—
## The Essential Elements
## Necessary to MASSIVELY Profit From Your List

# CHAPTER 15

## Treat Your Subscribers Like People and Show Them You Care

Relationships are necessary in order to turn your subscribers into paying customers. Before they will ever consider buying from you, they must first know, like and trust you. Which is why you must develop one-to-one relationships.

Ezines are all about 'one-to-one' marketing. So don't think of your subscribers as just subscribers. Think of them as people. People—who are YOUR customers. If you treat them well, they will be your customers for life.

One-to-one marketing is relationship marketing. That means your job is to continually build and foster your relationship with your subscribers. As your relationship builds, so will the trust and loyalty your subscribers have for you.

As their trust in and loyalty to you grows, you create an increasing amount of 'permission' to sell them your products—products that provide solutions to their problems.

To learn more about permission marketing, I suggest reading Seth Godin's book, *Permission Marketing*. It taught me a great deal about how to build relationships with my customers.

## Become an Expert

The one-to-one relationship you want to establish is an expert-to-novice relationship. (Hint: you're the expert.)

Think about it. If you had an option to purchase from an average Joe or an expert in the field of your interest, which one are you going to buy from?

The expert, of course.

So it is of utmost importance that you position yourself as an expert in your field. The good news is that you're already an expert. (Didn't know that, did you?) Your newsletter is the reason I can declare you an expert without personally knowing you.

If you're writing a newsletter or sending out regular messages to your subscribers related to a certain topic, you obviously know a lot about that topic. So call yourself an expert. Your subscribers probably see you as an expert anyway, since you are sending them regular email messages.

You can enhance that positioning by doing a number of things. One such thing is to write articles.

By writing articles that are getting published all over the Internet, people learn to view you as an expert in your field because you are offering advice within a certain niche.

The next step up from writing articles is writing a book. If you become a published author, people automatically see you as an authority figure. If you were to write a book that becomes a number one bestseller, how much more authority or level of expertise are people going to attach to you?

Aside from writing, public speaking is a great way to have people view you as an authority or an expert in your field. So seek opportunities to speak at seminars, workshops and events in your niche.

An easier way, perhaps, is to align yourself with other experts. You could do this by interviewing other experts in your related field. Or you can go to seminars and workshops and get your photograph taken with those experts. Just be sure to include those photos on your website for your visitors and subscribers to see.

When they see you with an expert, they learn to associate you with that expert. That expert's credibility then instantly gets transferred to you.

## Be Real:
## Show And Tell

Although you do want your list to view you as an expert, you also want them to see you as a real person.

When you have a relationship with another person, you often tell stories about your own personal life. So do the same with your opt-in email list. Share some personal information about yourself with your subscribers. Let them know who you are without being overly polished or corporate-sounding.

People do not like perfect or polished or corporate personas. People like individuals they can relate to and connect with. Consequently, you need to offer them something they can connect with so they can see you are just like them.

Take my friend Matt Bacak. He has a weekly video he sends to his subscribers called "Matt's Messy Desk." On that video clip, Matt talks with his subscribers and tells them a little story. Usually that story has some sort of marketing or sales message. Or perhaps it has a lesson tied to it so that they're learning something from the message.

More importantly, he's titled it "Matt's Messy Desk." That way, when people watch this video, they see Matt as he truly is. They see him standing there unshaven in his shorts and t-shirt in front of his messy desk.

What Matt is doing here is showing his subscribers that he is a real person just like them.

When people understand that you are a real person, they are more apt to identify with you. If they can identify with you, they're probably going to like you. If they like you, there's a better chance they're going to buy from you.

So don't try to make a website or create a persona that is overly polished or big and corporate-feeling.

It may end up biting you in the butt.

This is why it's very important that you focus on similarities. People tend to like others who are like themselves. The more you can connect with a person, the greater the likelihood that they will say yes to you. So try to uncover commonalities between you and your prospect.

Both blogging and teleseminars are great ways to show you are real, because blogging and teleseminars allow you the opportunity to share more information about yourself on a personal level than typical marketing mediums do.

When sharing information about yourself, people have an opportunity to identify with you in some way, shape, or form. They may find some similarities in your stories to things in their own lives. As they find those similarities or commonalities, they will learn to know, like and trust you more.

## Be an Expert Who Cares

Let's recap.

You've established yourself as an expert while demonstrating to your subscribers that you are just like them.

Now you need to show them you care about them.

How do you show people you don't know and have never met that you care without sounding cheesy or trite or false?

Easy. Solicit their feedback.

Ask your subscribers what they want. Ask them what their problems are. Ask them how you can help them.

Feedback is the most important thing you can get from your subscribers. If you know what they want, what their needs are, and how you can help them, all you have to do is create a solution that solves their problems.

Another benefit of feedback is that it reminds you that you're not just writing to email addresses.

When real people with real problems respond to your questions, you start to build real relationships with the unique personalities behind those emails addresses.

In your newsletter emails, constantly solicit feedback. In every message, ask some version of the following questions:

"How can I help you?"

"Is there anything you need from me?"

"What do you want?"

"What do you need?"

But because you've taken action on all the list-building techniques in Part II of this book, you've got a huge list. That huge list is generating a lot of responses.

How are you supposed to organize all that data from all those responses?

I've got a solution for you: <u>PagePersonalizer.com</u>.

If you recall, Page Personalizer automatically personalizes and customizes your Web pages to show your visitor's name and interests right on your Web page. Additionally, this program has a function that allows you to create surveys.

You can create a survey that asks your subscribers what their most important question is regarding _____ (whatever your area of expertise).

When they fill out and submit the form, their data is directly inputted into your Page Personalizer account. From there, you can sort through the data and find out what the most important and common questions (problems) are that your subscribers have.

Once you have that information, you demonstrate your expertise to your list by providing a solution to their problems. You can create your own solution or find another product that somebody else is already selling on the Internet and become an affiliate for that product.

That wraps up the lesson in relationship marketing, so you now know how to treat your subscribers—err, I mean customers. What you need to learn next is how to sell them what they *want*.

# CHAPTER 16

## How to Develop
## Gushing Rivers of Never-Ending Cash

If you only want a list of subscribers who view you as an expert and with whom you have a solid relationship, I give you permission to stop reading because you now have all the information you need to accomplish that goal.

BUT... if you want to turn those subscribers into customers, this is the time to focus. This is the part of the book you absolutely must give your undivided attention to.

So turn off the TV.

Ignore the ringing phone.

Close the door.

It's time for you to learn how to make massive amounts of money.

### Digital Products = Passive Income

Joining affiliate programs is a great way to develop passive income streams. But you're not content with just having streams; you want gushing rivers of passive income.

That means you need to have your own product or service to sell.

The best thing to sell on the Internet is a digitally delivered product or service. Examples include: ebooks (electronic books), courses, membership sites and software.

People surfing the Internet want instant gratification.

Digitally delivered products and services provide this instant gratification because they can be accessed or downloaded immediately upon online credit card payment. This is not possible with items that require shipping.

Furthermore, digitally delivered products and services cost little to produce and have the potential to yield never-ending revenue. Once you have your site completed and your product or services ready, you incur no additional costs.

The product or service is created once, then sold and resold. Such products and services have no overhead, don't require storage space and have no shipping charges.

You create it once and sell it forever!

The key to developing a digital product is to 'sell your knowledge.' What do you know that others could benefit from?

Are you a great cook? Then put together an ebook on cooking.

Are you an artist? Then sell an online course teaching how to paint and draw.

Are you a mom? Then sell a members-only mom site that tells everything you know about infant care.

If you're still not sure what to create, answer the following questions:

What do people seek your advice about?

What hobbies do you have?

If you're successful in your career, how did you become successful?

What are you passionate about?

Write all your thoughts down without editing them. Once you have a list of about ten ideas, start to work through them. You'll be amazed at what you know about certain subjects.

## How to Create Your Very Own Products And Services That Will Have Your Readers Begging to Buy From You

Okay, what I am about to share with you can be worth hundreds of thousands of dollars if you use and apply it...

Actually, we just talked about it a few pages ago...

It was important then, but it's critical now...

Here it is, the best way to determine your customers' wants and needs... Ask them.

That's it! You've just uncovered one of the best-kept sales secrets known to mankind. But here's the thing. Most people don't do it because it's so simple.

Don't make things more difficult than they have to be. The fact is that all you need to do to create your very own products and services that will have your readers begging to buy from you is ask them what they want and sell it to them.

How else can you determine *exactly* what your subscribers, prospects or customers actually want? You can't.

*The only way that you can determine exactly what they want is to ask them.*

As I mentioned before, you can use <u>PagePersonalizer.com</u> to organize the responses you get when you ask your subscribers what they want.

It is also a great tool for building your list and your business.

Essentially, what it does is ask your customers or prospects what their most important question is regarding _____. When they enter their question, they also enter their name and their email address.

When they click the submit button, they're added to your list. So you are creating a targeted list, because you know what their needs are. They're telling you in their question.

All of this information (name, email, question) goes into the your database. Within the database, you can sort through all the questions people ask of you. You can, thus, determine what the most common questions are, what the most popular questions are and what the burning issues or problems are that your prospects have.

Since you know what this targeted list wants, finding out what to sell them is like shooting fish in a barrel. Their questions are the answer!

If you don't already have the product or the service that they want, create it.

But you only have to create it if you want to make money.

## How to Instantly Make Money From Your List Just Seconds After People Subscribe

Do you know that you can make money immediately after acquiring a new subscriber?

All you need to do is utilize the power of the 'Thank You' page, which is perhaps the most valuable piece of Web real estate you own.

This is the page that people are redirected to after taking some sort of action on your website: subscribing to your newsletter, making a purchase or submitting a feedback form.

As you may have guessed, this page should thank your subscribers and acknowledge them for the action they just took. It's the only polite thing to do; and didn't your mother always teach you to be polite?

More importantly, though, this page is a prime opportunity for you to up-sell or cross-sell your visitor with related products or services.

Keep in mind that this is a time when you have already 'sold' them once on the previous page. Why not try again, while they are still in the 'buying' mode? This is often referred to as the 'Yes' momentum because the more you can get people to say yes, the more the they will continue to with greater ease each time.

The key is that the offer must be relevant to what they just subscribed to.

For example, if your subscriber has just subscribed to your newsletter on how to build a highly responsive opt-in email list, offer them an immediate solution like this book or a teleseminar or a home study course.

If they buy, you can then try up-selling or cross-selling.

This is simply good manners. If they want to buy more of what you have to offer, it's your job to give them that chance.

The worst that can happen is that they leave your page feeling good for being thanked, acknowledged and appreciated.

Generally, up-selling means to sell a customer a higher priced version of a product or service.

McDonald's offers a prime example of up-selling. How many times have you heard this question: "Would you like to super size your meal?"

However, it can also mean buying something in addition to what you have purchased. So if a customer just bought an audio program, you could ask, "Would you like to buy the transcripts to go along with the audio you just purchased?"

On the other hand, cross-selling means selling a different, but related product or service. For example, when you buy insurance for your car, the salesperson will often ask if you would like to buy home insurance, too.

To see the difference between up-selling and cross-selling, let's say you're selling an audio recording of a private interview with an expert for $97.00.

Immediately after your customer buys the audio recording, you could up-sell with the transcripts to the interview, or you could cross-sell with a second interview of another expert.

So be polite. Always thank your subscribers.

# CHAPTER 17

## Just Because the Mail Man Delivers Rain or Shine Doesn't Mean Your Email Server Will

As a success-minded email marketer, you've done everything you need to do.

You've established a one-to-one relationship with your list.

You've asked them their problems and created a solution.

Now you're ready to deliver the product that will make your subscribers' hopes and dreams come true.

But your message is blocked.

Marked as spam.

Now you have a problem... you can't deliver your solution!

That's why understanding how to avoid spam accusations is important to the success of your business.

## How To Avoid SPAM Accusations And Get Your Messages Whitelisted

Let's start with the basics.

You can acquire two main types of subscribers: single opt-in and double opt-in.

Single opt-in implies permission. This means someone has given you explicit permission to send them an email in some capacity. They give this permission by entering in their first name and email address, then clicking on the submit button.

Double opt-in takes this process one step further. After the individual enters his first name and email address and clicks submit, he is sent a confirmation email.

In that email, he is asked to click on a link to confirm that he does, in fact, want to be subscribed to your newsletter. He only becomes a subscriber of your ezine after clicking on that link.

I personally recommend acquiring only double opt-in subscribers. They are more valuable than single-opt in subscribers for three reasons.

One, the confirmation email gives the subscriber a chance to verify that he does, indeed, want to receive your newsletter. His subscribing was not an error.

Two, the confirmation email makes it difficult for people to subscribe their buddies. In other words, if Joe subscribes Bill to your newsletter and Bill receives a confirmation email, Bill can then choose whether or not he wants to be subscribed to your newsletter.

In a single opt-in process, this would not happen. Bill would inadvertently be subscribed to your newsletter even though he didn't actually request to be on your list.

The third thing the confirmation email does is confirm that the entered email address is valid. Because a confirmation email message is sent to the address the subscriber entered into the Web form on your subscription page, he will not receive the message if the address is invalid. Thus, you are not stuck with a bunch of 'dead' email addresses.

Moving on.

When your double-opt in subscriber clicks the link in the confirmation email, he's added to your list and sent the first message in your sequential autoresponder series.

Your first email message is often called a 'Thank You' message. To avoid being accused of spamming, use this message to both thank your subscribers, and tell them when and where they subscribed to your newsletter. This is also a courtesy to remind them that they did, in fact, request to be subscribed to your newsletter and where they subscribed to it.

You'll also need to include an unsubscribe link at the bottom of every message you send out.

This is a link that subscribers can click on if they choose that they no longer want to be subscribed to your newsletter. As soon as they click on that link, they will be removed from your mailing list.

The other thing you should include at the bottom of your email messages is your name and mailing address.

Finally, be sure to only send relevant and requested information. If somebody has signed up for your healthy recipes newsletter, do not send them messages on Internet marketing.

Doing these things will greatly help you avoid any type of spam complaints or accusations.

A word of warning, though. Just because your first email got through doesn't mean the rest of the messages in your autoresponder will get to your subscribers. So you need to have your subscribers 'whitelist' your email address.

The best way to explain this is to show you how I do it. Below is the actual copy that I use on one of my 'Thank You' pages.

## How to Make Sure You Get Our Email

Increasingly, ISPs are using filtering systems to try and keep Spam out of customers' inboxes. Sometimes, they accidentally filter the email that you want to receive.

To make sure that your List Builder subscriber reports and support emails are not filtered into your "junk" or "bulk" folder, please add List Builder to your list of trusted senders. Here's how:

Hotmail: Place the domains GlenHopkins.name and ListOpt.com on your safe list, so that you can receive our emails. Also, please place support@ListOpt.com, subscribers@ ListOpt.com, billing@ListOpt.com and Glen@ListOpt.com on your safe list, so you can receive our support replies. The safe list can be accessed via the "Options" link next to the main menu tabs.

AOL: Place the domains GlenHopkins.name and ListOpt.com and support@ListOpt.com, subscribers@ListOpt.com, billing@ListOpt.com and Glen@ListOpt.com in your address book.

Yahoo! Mail: If one of our emails is filtered to your 'bulk' folder, open the message and click on the "this is not Spam" link next to the "From" field.

Some spam filters: Place the domains GlenHopkins.name and ListOpt.com and support@ListOpt.com, subscribers@ListOpt.com, billing@ListOpt.com and Glen@ListOpt.com on the filter's whitelist. You may need to search a filter's help to determine how to do this.

Other ISPs: If one of your List Builder related emails is being filtered, try adding our domains GlenHopkins.name and ListOpt.com or our email's 'From' or 'Reply-to' address to your address book or contact list. If this option is not available, try moving the message to your 'inbox' or forwarding the message to yourself.

If subsequent messages continue to be filtered, call or email your ISP's tech support and specifically ask how you can be sure to receive all email from GlenHopkins.name and ListOpt.com and support@ListOpt.com, subscribers@ListOpt.com, billing@ListOpt.com and Glen@ListOpt.com. Follow their instructions for whitelisting.

Thank you in advance for taking the time to do this. Sorry for the inconvenience, but these circumstances are beyond our control. All you, and we can do, is work together with the ISPs to shut out the spammers.

Thank You!

Glen Hopkins

## Spam-Check Your Ezine Messages

Just getting whitelisted won't solve all your deliverability issues, though.

Nope.

You also need to spam-check your ezine messages.

Spam is growing into a bigger and bigger problem. Yet while spam is the fundamental root of the problem, the anti-spam measures that large ISP's and important free email hosts (like Hotmail and Yahoo! Mail) undertake are what hurts legitimate email marketers like us.

Much like tuna nets catch dolphins by mistake, their spam filters catch us. That's why I use the SiteSell SpamCheck Tool. It's a quick way for honest marketers to make sure that their emails are less likely to be considered spam by ISP's, by Yahoo! Mail and Hotmail.

Here's how SiteSell SpamCheck works:

1. In the subject line, type TEST in uppercase, then copy-and-paste your actual subject. (If the subject does NOT start with TEST, it assumes the message is REAL spam and deletes it.) Here's a sample subject: TESTFlower-Lovers Ezine #007: Peonies for the Yukon.

2. Copy-and-paste the rest of your ezine message into the body section of the email and send it to spam-check-lop@SiteSell.net.

3. Wait for your reply message.

You'll get a report back (in seconds, perhaps a few minutes if volume is heavy) telling you how good or bad your email is from a spam-detector's point of view.

This reply includes a full, free report of all corrections that you should make to your ezine message if you want it to stay out of the junk folders.

It does NOT, of course, comment on WHAT you write. First, it's not that smart, and second, the actual content is YOUR business.

# CHAPTER 18

## Curiosity May Kill Cats,
## But it Gets Readers to Open Email

Hooray!

Your message got through the anti-spam battlefield and is sitting in your subscriber's inbox.

So that means you can take a deep breath, relax and wait for the money to start pouring in, right?

Wrong.

People's inboxes are inundated with hundreds upon hundreds of email messages, messages from friends, family, colleagues, marketers and spammers.

So how do you get your message to stand out from the crowd?

By grabbing attention with a well-crafted headline/subject line.

## How to Write Subject Lines
## That Stand Out From The Crowd
### And Intrigue Your Readers So Much
### That They Can't Wait to Open Your Messages

To help draw attention to your email, the first step you should take is to use your name in the 'From' field. You should never use Admin or Support or your website name. Your emails are always 'from' your name.

For example, whenever somebody receives an email from me, the 'From' always says 'Glen Hopkins.' I do this because I want that person to know the message is coming from me, and because I want to brand my name. When people see my name, they recognize it immediately.

The other thing you should do is put a hyphen on either side of your name, like this: (- Glen Hopkins -).

By doing this, the hyphen forces your message to be displayed at the top of all other email messages, assuming, of course, that subscribers view their inboxes by sorting messages using the 'From' sort.

So you've got your name at the top of the inbox.

Use your subscriber's name in the subject line. The more personalization you can use in the subject line, the greater your open rate will be for the messages that you send.

Whenever it makes sense, include your subscriber's first name. If possible, include other personal information, such as the name of their city, the product they purchased from you, the date of the purchase, etc.

You also want to make the subject line as intriguing as possible. Peak the reader's curiosity. The goal is to get them from reading the subject line to opening and reading your email.

Hint: one of the greatest ways of doing this is to ask a question. People naturally want to know the answer.

To help you, here are some sample subject lines:

*Hi Joe, it's me, Glen.*

*Joe, Did You Hear What's Happening Tonight?*

*I Shouldn't Be Telling You This, Joe...*

*Did You Get Your Copy, Joe?*

*Joe, 3 Secrets to Building a Huge List.*

*Joe, Part 4 of 5 is Ready.*

*Can You Make it to New York, Joe?*

*Joe, Meet Me in New York?*

*You're Not Going to Believe This, Joe...*

*Joe, This is Your Last Chance.*

*I Don't Normally Do This, Joe.*

Here's something else to keep in mind when writing subject lines: curiosity may kill cats, but it gets your subscribers to open emails.

# CHAPTER 19

## Mind Control Marketing

You've built a relationship by giving information, asking questions and sharing stories about yourself.

You've found or created a product your customers want.

You've gotten your subscribers to whitelist your email address, and you've spam-proofed your sales message.

You've delivered your message to your subscribers' inbox and written a killer subject line they can't wait to open.

In other words, it's time to let your customers buy what they've told you they want.

However, sending a sales message that reads, "Here's my product. Buy it," is not going to generate any sales. You still have to persuade your customers to buy, even if you know your product is exactly what they requested you provide for them.

Notice I said, persuade. Not trick or connive or take advantage of—persuade.

Because human psychology is closely tied to the sales and marketing process, you need to have a basic understanding of the psychological principles of persuasion in order to convert prospects into customers.

By understanding and applying these principles, you will be in a much better position to succeed.

Below, I will discuss some of the basic principles and how you can apply them to your marketing. For a more in depth understanding, I recommend reading *INFLUENCE: The Psychology of Persuasion* by Robert Cialdini, PH.D.

## Reciprocity

When somebody gives us something, whether it is a gift or a favor, we feel indebted to them. We feel that we must give back, so we'll say, "Much obliged," instead of "Thank you." When we say, "Much obliged," what we're really saying is, "I am obligated to repay you." We feel a sense of obligation.

That is reciprocity.

You can use this phenomenon in a number of ways in your sales and marketing efforts. By being the first to give something, you create a sense of obligation in the gift-receiver to repay you.

To start the reciprocal process, offer your subscribers a free report.

Or upgrade them to a gold account at no charge, if they sign-up for a basic account.

Give them an ebook.

Provide them valuable content or "how to" information.

Offer them a free teleseminar.

All of these are possible gifts that you can give your subscribers. As you give them valuable information, content, products, and resources, they naturally develop a sense of obligation to repay you because you have done them a favor.

So when you make a sales offer, they are more willing to buy from you.

Why?

Well, not only are they interested in the product that you're selling, but they also want the opportunity to do something nice for you. And their way of doing something nice for you, is to buy the product or service you're selling.

## Over-Deliver

How do you feel when you purchase a product or service, and it or the merchant *exceeds* your expectations?

Doesn't that *feel* great?

Do you feel as though you made the *right* choice in buying from that merchant?

Do you *like* the merchant more now?

Would you be more apt to offer repeat business or tell your friends?

Such is the power that comes from over-delivering.

When you give more than your customers are expecting, it helps you develop the *relationship* with them. Chances are they will like you more and look upon you with more favor than before. In fact, they may even look upon you with more favor than they look on your competition.

Smart companies and business people do their best to exceed customer expectations. The key is to give something above and beyond what you have that has a high perceived value to your customer, but low financial value to you.

How can you over-deliver?

One way, is to own the master resale rights to any digital product. If you don't currently own some, you can buy them. You'll only have to pay for them once. Then you can sell them or give them away as often as you like—at no additional cost.

To demonstrate, let's say you own the master resale rights to a piece of software—an audio interview, a special report or some other downloadable digital product that could easily sell, for say $97.00.

Therefore, the product is seen as highly valuable to your customer.

It costs nothing for you to give away.

Think about what digital product or service you can give to your subscribers or customers as a bonus or *unexpected* bonus that would cost you next to nothing. Then give it away and become known as someone who over-delivers.

## Scarcity

Opportunities seem more valuable to us when availability is limited. In fact, studies show that people are more motivated by the thought of 'losing' something than by the thought of 'gaining' something.

Scarcity can be used well in conjunction with quantity and time.

For example, a marketing message using the scarcity of quantity might say:

"This email was sent out to over 100,000 subscribers, but only the first 100 to respond will get this amazing widget for 50% off!"

On the other hand, a marketing message employing the scarcity of time might say:

"Get 50% off this amazing widget today only. Buy before 5 p.m. or pay double the price!"

A third option is to combine both the scarcity of quantity AND time:

*"Only 100 widgets available.*

*The first 25 people to buy get it for just $47.*

*The first 26 to 75 people to buy get it for $97.*

*The first 76 to 100 people to buy get it for $147.*

Once all 100 widgets are sold, they will never be made available again!"

But perhaps the best use of the principle of scarcity is the One-Time Offer.

A one-time offer is typically presented on a 'Thank You' page. It is a special offer that is available to the reader at that very moment, one time only. If they choose not to purchase the offer right then, they will never again be given the opportunity.

As you can imagine, one-time offers have a strong psychological effect on the reader. They feel that if they do not act immediately, they will lose out on the deal of a lifetime. Nobody wants to feel like a loser.

Note: whenever you set a limited offer in terms of time or quantity, always stick to it. If you tell people that your offer is only available to the first 100 buyers who buy before midnight June 10th, then don't extend your offer to the 101st person, or to a person asking to get the deal on June 11th.

If you do, you will lose credibility. Your customers will simply dismiss you in the future when you tell them something is available for a limited time or in a limited quantity.

By sticking to your deadlines, another thing happens: you train your customers to buy when you tell them to buy.

If they missed out once, the next time you have a limited time or quantity sale, your customers will come running to buy from you for fear that they may lose out again.

## Reason Why

Have you ever noticed that children are constantly asking one question: "Why?"

They want a reason for everything. And here's a little secret: we never grow out of the need to know why.

Studies have shown that you can double the likelihood that a person will buy from you if you give them a reason why. Interestingly, these studies also show that even silly or invalid reasons will increase your response rate. Ultimately, however, the more valid and believable your reason, the better your response rate will be.

Any reason whatsoever will increase the chances that people will buy from you, because it satisfies that instinctual need to know why.

It is, therefore, imperative that you always include one vital word in your sales copy. That word is *because.*

All you need to do is add because to the end of your sentence. *Purchase this product today because _____.*

*Do it now because _____.*

Give your subscriber a reason why they should buy from you.

## Social Proof

Often, we determine what is correct based on what other people think or say is correct. In fact, the larger the number of other people that say something is correct, the more we tend to agree.

Recognize any of these marketing messages?

"Over A Billion Served."—McDonald's

"The pain reliever hospitals use most."—Tylenol

"When monitoring a patient after open heart surgery, the brand of battery that hospitals trust most is Duracell."—Duracell

Each message focuses on how many people use their product. Duracell even ties in a second psychological trigger called 'Authority.'

## Authority

When you walk into a doctor's office, have you ever noticed the plaques and awards hanging on the wall for you to see and admire?

Or have you noticed the plaques and awards posted on the wall of your auto body shop as you wait for your car to be repaired?

Doctors and mechanics and other professionals do this because it gives you the perception that they do, indeed, know what they are doing and that they are authorities in their field.

When you go to them for help, you know you are getting expert advice. People love to get advice from experts. They are obedient to people in authority.

For this reason, you want to show your credentials whenever possible.

For example, if you have a Doctorate, you would include the Ph. D. at the end of your name on your business cards. Also, posting pictures on your website of awards, plaques or certificates that you might have received is a great way to show your level of expertise.

People will learn to perceive you as an authority in your field. If you're the author of a book—especially if it's a #1 best-selling book—you should advertise that on your website as well.

## Endorsements

Celebrity endorsements are everywhere. Companies pay celebrities big bucks in order to endorse their products because they know that people who are well known, and 'liked' by the general public, transfer their credibility to the product.

- Singer Beyonce Knowles signed a huge endorsement deal with L'Oreal.

- Justin Timberlake signed a $6 million deal to promote the McDonald's "I'm Lovin' It" tag line.

- Robert De Niro is doing American Express ads.

Don't worry. I'm not suggesting you sign multi-million dollar deals with celebrities you probably can't get access to anyway.

You don't need celebrities, because people who are well known and respected in your field, have the same effect as celebrities.

Determine who those people are and ask them if they would be interested in giving your product or service a try. Consider giving them a free sample or membership, and then solicit their feedback.

If they liked your product or service, ask them for a testimonial. Then post it predominantly on your website and in your sales copy.

Don't forget to ask your existing customers for their feedback. With their approval, their feedback can often times be used as a testimonial.

When you do receive testimonials, keep in mind that the best ones should include the following key elements:

- A headline.
- A photo of the person.
- The person's name, address and website.
- An audio message from the person.

Here's an example.

Click to
Listen

## "John Smith Is My Secret Weapon"

*"For the last three years I have been coached by the best in the business, John Smith. The strategies that John has helped me to understand and employ in my own business have taken me from zero to mega profits in just 60 days!"*

*William Watson*
*www.williamsdomain.com*
*City, State, Country*

## Contrast

Contrast is nothing more than helping your prospects realize the value in your product or service compared to another product or service that they are already sold on.

For example, let's assume your prospect is a coffee drinker and the widget you are selling costs $29.00 per month. You might say:

*"For less than a measly dollar a day, this amazing widget quickly and easily does blah, blah, blah, helping you earn more and work less. Under a buck a day—that's less than you pay for your daily cup of coffee!"*

How can you use the principle of contrast in your sales copy?

## Liking

Most people prefer to interact and deal with people that they know and like, so try to find some similarity between you and your prospect.

Maybe you both like baseball.
Maybe you both have kids in the third grade.
Maybe you both love Thai food.

Whatever it is, find it. When a prospect can identify with you based on some similarity, he is more apt to like you and, thus, buy from you.

You should also look for opportunities to praise people and use their names. In his book, *How To Win Friends And Influence People*, Dale Carnegie says:

"We should be aware of the magic contained in a name and realize that this single item is wholly and completely owned by the person with whom we are dealing... and nobody else."

"The name sets the individual apart; it makes him or her unique among all others. The information we are imparting or the request we are making takes on a special importance when we approach the situation with the name of the individual. From the waitresses to the senior executives, *the name will work magic as we deal with others.*"

"Remember that a person's name is, to that person, the sweetest and most important sound in any language."

If you have never read Carnegie's book, I highly recommend you do.

## Emotion: Want vs. Need

If you had the choice to sell your subscribers something they wanted or something they needed, which would you choose?

You would choose the product they need because they have to buy it, right?

Well, yes and no.

Just because your subscribers need a product doesn't mean they want it. In fact, the opposite is often true; they don't want it, but out of necessity, are required to purchase it.

That means they're spending money on a requirement rather than a desire, so they become resistant to your sales messages. And because they resist spending their money on something they don't necessarily want, it can become very difficult to sell it to them.

Take auto insurance, for example.

If you want to drive a vehicle, you are required by law to own automobile insurance. Just because you are required to purchase it, does not mean you want to purchase it.

Perhaps you don't see the value in it or you don't understand the value of it.

In any case, many people do not want to spend their hard-earned dollars on something that they do not want, such as auto insurance. So, they shop around looking for one thing only—the best price. It, thus, becomes difficult for an auto insurance sales person to sell insurance policies.

On the other hand, let's say you sell cars, and Jack comes to you to buy a car. After speaking with him for a few minutes, you learn he is interested in the red sports car. You know this car costs twice as much as one of the more 'practical' cars on the lot, but you also know it's not the car that Jack wants.

Chances are, what Jack wants is the status that comes from owning such a car. So you paint a mental picture for him of how great he'll feel when he's driving down the road with the top down, waving at his friends and family and colleagues.

You don't sell him what he needs (a car); you sell him what he wants (feeling great and important and proud).

Whatever his reasons, it is your job to uncover his personal desires. As you take him through the sales process, you constantly reinforce those emotions, and remind him of the benefits he receives from purchasing that car.

Take a look around your house at all of your possessions and you'll quickly discover that almost everything you own, you purchased based on emotion rather than out of necessity.

Therefore take the time to find out exactly what it is your subscribers and customers want. Focus on selling them what they want, not what they need.

## Supercharge Messages with Multiple Persuasion Tactics

Do you have to use just one principle of persuasion per sales message?

NO!

Use as many as you can, like in this example, of a woman praising her favorite salon:

*"My hairstylist Massimo was trained by the best in his motherland Italy (Authority). My good friend Sonia recommended him to me (Testimonial). He even cuts and styles the hair of several celebrities (Social Proof). He is in such demand that I have to book over a month in advance (Scarcity). But when I am there, he pampers me with wine and cheese. It's so relaxing (Reciprocity, Over-Deliver)."*

Basically, it comes down to this: emotion sells. That's why it is your job as a sales person to tap into the emotions of your subscribers and uncover the real reasons why your prospect wants your product or service.

Persuade your subscribers to buy, and you will end up with a huge, highly profitable opt-in email list.

# PART IV

## Tying It All Together

# CHAPTER 20

## The Grand Conclusion

You now have all the knowledge and tools necessary to build a huge, highly profitable opt-in email list. The key to your success will be taking the time to actually apply and put into action what you have learned.

### Oh, the Knowledge You've Gained

You've learned that success begins in your mind, and you can accomplish anything—if you don't let fear control you.

You've learned that your list is your ticket to business survival, even if your marketplace totally disappears.

You've learned that starting and running a successful email marketing business can be accomplished in six steps:

1. Select and Purchase a Domain Name.

2. Find a Hosting Service to Host Your Website.

3. Automate Your Business with an Autoresponder.

4. Set Up a Squeeze Page.

5. Create a Sales Page.

6. Follow-up with Sequential Sales Messages.

You've learned that the top ten secrets of lucrative list building are:
1. Squeeze Pages
2. Signature Files and Business Cards
3. Viral Marketing
4. Articles
5. Search Engine Traffic
6. Ezine Advertising
7. MasterMind Groups and Joint Ventures
8. Affiliate Programs
9. Teleseminars
10. Co-registration

You've learned that the one-to-one relationship is the vital element of email marketing.

You've learned that you need to position yourself as an expert who cares to develop that one-to-one relationship.

You've learned that creating products your customers want is as easy as asking them what they want and then giving it to them.

You've learned that email deliverability is unreliable because of the spam filters, so you've learned ways to get through those filters.

You've learned that writing intriguing subject lines gets subscribers to open their email and read your messages.

You've learned that mind control marketing plays a crucial role in persuading your customers to buy from you.

You've learned how to implement the following persuasion tactics in your sales messages:
• Reciprocity
• Over-deliver
• Scarcity
• Reason Why
• Social Proof
• Authority

- Endorsements
- Contrast
- Liking
- Emotion: Want vs. Need

And you've learned that above all, emotion sells.

## What to Do with All Your Knowledge

Now that you have all this knowledge, the first thing you need to do is set specific goals to determine exactly what it is you want to accomplish.

Then you must take massive action on a consistent, persistent basis in order to succeed.

Think of it like building muscles. The first time you walk into a gym, chances are you will not be able to bench press 250 lbs. However, if you are persistent and consistently weight train at the gym, you will find yourself getting stronger and closer to your goal with each and every visit.

You will, however, notice roadblocks on your journey towards your goals. That is, you will encounter obstacles that seem to jump out of nowhere in an attempt to halt your progress.

Count on these obstacles.

They are a part of life. Everyone would have every success they ever wanted if there were no obstacles.

Your job is to be persistent and work through those obstacles. If you find little or no obstacles along the way, chances are you are not really challenging yourself.

So when you do reach your goal, you won't experience the feeling of 'sweet success.'

Make your goal a challenging one!

If you take the time to study any successful person, you learn that the vast majority of them have had more 'failures' than they have had 'successes.'

This is because successful people are persistent; the more they stumble and fall, the more they get right back up and get going again.

On the other hand, people that don't get back up and try again, never reach success.

Walt Disney was turned down 302 times before he got financing for his dream of creating the "Happiest Place on Earth." Today, due to his persistence, millions of people have shared 'the joy of Disney.'

Colonel Sanders spent two years driving across the United States looking for restaurants to buy his chicken recipe. He was turned down 1,009 times!

How successful is Kentucky Fried Chicken today?

Having said this, keep in mind that you must constantly re-evaluate your circumstances and the approach you are using to reach your goal. There is no sense in being persistent at something that you are doing incorrectly.

Sometimes you have to modify your approach along the way. Every time you do something, learn from it and find a better way to do it the next time.

Today is the day to begin your journey to building a huge, highly profitable opt-in email list.

Be consistent and persistent and you will succeed!

—*Glen Hopkins*

# "BUT WAIT, THERE'S MORE!"

# APPENDIX I

## How to Write
## Professional Ad Copy that Works

Whether you're writing short ads or long sales letters, you need to be able to write 'killer' sales copy.

Sending out a few words in your ezine WILL NOT generate sales unless you know how to write the ad well.

So how do you write killer sales copy? You have three choices:

1. Write it yourself.
2. Hire a professional copywriter.
3. Write it yourself with the help of professional writing tools.

Writing it yourself is cheap, but not wise if you haven't studied copywriting. Sure, it won't cost you anything to produce, but you are not likely to generate any sales.

Hiring a professional will produce results, but can cost you many thousands of dollars.

That's why I suggest option number three: write it yourself with the help of professional writing tools. That's also how I do it, and the writing tool that helps me is LucrativeListBuilding.com/saleslettersoftware/.

By combining the power of Sales Letter Software with the following knowledge, you'll be able to produce professional sales copy without actually having to pay out huge sums of money.

Let's get right to it, shall we? The following is a break down of the do's and don'ts of effective ad writing.

Don't...

- Use too many exclamation points!!!!! This gives the perception of 'hype,' and hype decreases credibility.
- Feel like you have to use all the space the publishers give you for ads. (Most allow 50 to 60 characters per line and seven–ten lines.) Blank white space helps make your ad 'jump off' the page.
- Make your URL too long. Long URL's scare readers and look ugly. If you have a long URL, create a shorter redirect URL. This gives you a more professional look.
- Let your URL split two lines (if it must be long). The reader will be forced to re-type it into their browser. Since readers don't want to do this, your response rate decreases. Always make getting to you as easy as possible for your prospects.
- Try to sell your product to the reader with your ad. The only purpose of your ad should be to get your reader interested enough to take the next step, such as visiting your site to get the free trial sample. Build the relationship with your customer from there. Eventually, it will lead to the 'big' sale as well as loyalty to you, and to your product or service.

Do...

- Identify yourself and your company with a real email address and URL. Customers like to know who they are dealing with. Would you prefer to buy from a real person with an identity (Glen@ListOpt.com) or an alias (ww3625ma@hotmail.com) who has no identity?
- Give your credentials and testimonials. While testimonials are obviously too long to put in your ezine ad, it is a good idea to create a page on your site dedicated to testimonials. If you want, you can place a link in your ad to this page.

- Use headlines to capture your reader's attention. If you don't get your reader's attention, the rest of the message is lost.
- Use spacing, bullets and centering throughout the body. White space helps your ad stand out.
- Use simple, direct speech. Write the way you would talk to a friend, because the average person reads at a grade seven level, big, fancy words are not good.
- Use the AIM Formula:
  **A** is for capturing attention.
  **I** is for creating interest.
  **M** is for motivation to act.

## The AIM Formula Explained

## A:Capture attention.

Treat the first sentence of your ad like a headline. Use it to grab the reader's attention.

Imagine the front page of a newspaper having no headlines. What are the chances of you being attracted to a particular article?

Test yourself. Grab the front page of a paper and cover all the headlines with masking tape.

Does the paper grab your attention now? Probably not.

So how do you capture attention? Try asking the reader a question:

"Have you ever wished you could be your own boss?"

Because people instinctively want to answer questions, they read on.

Here are some common headlines. Modify them to suit your product or service:

- What if you knew who would win the Stanley Cup before the final game?
- Looking for a _____ that will _____?
- How to make _____ in less than 30 days.
- Are you prepared to _____ by _____?
- Have you noticed how many people _____?

## I: Create interest.

Once you have the reader's attention, focus on the benefits of your product or service.

How will it benefit your prospects?

The best way to do this is to tap into the emotions of the reader. People make emotional buying decisions, not logical ones.

Another way to create interest is to offer guarantees, testimonials and free samples.

The more bonuses you can offer, the better. Customers want the most they can possibly get without having to give too much up front.

## M: Motivate readers to act.

The call to action is the most critical aspect of the AIM formula.

If you've done your job by capturing attention and creating interest, you've created the momentum you need to motivate your readers to act. So tell them what you want them to do.

Here are some ways you can call your reader to immediate action:

- Create deadlines.
- Offer discounts for quick action.
- Limited availability.
- Offer bonuses.
- Contests, sweepstakes.
- Make it EASY for customers to respond.
- Remind the reader of benefits.

Whatever you do, ALWAYS ask the reader to act.

## Test Your Ad

Now that your ad is written and ready bring in customers, WAIT!

Before you invest in a large ad campaign, start with smaller test runs using multiple versions of your ad.

Test various target groups and newsletters. Track the responses you get on an ad and compare it to another ad for the same product or service.

It is amazing how slight changes in wording can dramatically affect your response rates.

Do be aware, though, that testing smaller versions of your ad means you'll have to pay more up front. However, once the testing is complete, you'll know what works and what doesn't. Use this knowledge to earn MUCH more in the future.

Based on your test results, create what you believe will be an effective ad and give it a try

## Some Final Things to Remember

Sales is all about presenting a solution to your customer that will solve their problem. Only poor salespeople try to sell their customers something they don't want or need.

Finally, check out PagePersonalizer.com to see an excellent example of a professional sales letter. A letter like this can be created in about 15 minutes using a Sales Letter Generator.

With software that creates sales letters, all you have to do is fill in the blanks, and generate professional sales copy instantly. To learn more about this service, visit: LucrativeListBuilding.com/saleslettersoftware/

Printed in the United States
55554LVS00004BA/190-306